Klondike Park

Klondike Park

From Seattle to Dawson City

Archie Satterfield

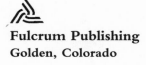

Fulcrum Publishing
Golden, Colorado

Copyright © 1993 Archie Satterfield
Cover design by Jody Chapel, Cover to Cover Design
Cover photos:
      Top—Lake Bennett, British Columbia, by Archie Satterfield
      Bottom—Stampeders on the summit of Chilkoot Pass circa 1898,
         copyright © 1993, Dedman's Photo Shop
Map on front cover by Kathleen Nichols Lanzoni
Interior maps by Ed Walker

Library of Congress Cataloging-in-Publication Data

Satterfield, Archie.
    Klondike Park : from Seattle to Dawson City / Archie Satterfield.
      p.   cm.
    Includes bibliographical references.
    ISBN 1-55591-165-X (paperback)
    1. Klondike Gold Rush National Historical Park (Alaska and Wash.)
—Guidebooks. 2. Klondike Gold Rush National Historical Park (Alaska
and Wash.)—History.   I. Title.
    F912.K56S27   1993
    979.8 ' 2—dc20   93-22928
                                                CIP

Printed in the United States of America
0 9 8 7 6 5 4 3 2 1

Fulcrum Publishing
350 Indiana Street, Suite 350
Golden, Colorado 80401-5093

For my grandsons, Christopher Adkins and Gus Hansen

Contents

Acknowledgments

This book was written with the cooperation and assistance of many people, some of whom I have known for more than twenty years. I hope that after they read the book they will feel the time they spent with me was not wasted.

In the U.S. National Park Service, I am particularly indebted to Willie Russell, Superintendent, and Marianne Mills, Chief Park Ranger, Klondike Gold Rush National Historical Park, Seattle Unit; Frank Norris, National Park Service historian in Anchorage; Clay Alderson, Superintendent, and Karl Gurcke, Resource Management Specialist in Skagway; and Glenn Hinsdale of the Pacific Northwest Regional office. I also want to thank Nita Nettleton, the ranger who was good company while I struggled up the summit of Chilkoot with knees that had aged eighteen years since the last crossing.

Also in Skagway, I would like to thank Steve Hites, formerly of the White Pass and Yukon Route, and Tina Cyr, who took over when Steve went into business for himself; Lori Sica and Jerre O'Farrell Fuqua of the Skagway Convention and Visitors Bureau; and Donna Whitehead of the Golden North Hotel.

I shall always be indebted to the late Bruce Harvey of the Canadian Parks Service, who loved the Klondike story more than most, and whose memory was insured when the mountain range overlooking Lake Bennett was named for him. More recently, I want to thank Bob Lewis, Canadian Parks Service's area superintendent of the Yukon National Historic Sites, and Rene Rivard, the warden on Chilkoot's summit whose hot lemonade made a cold and rainy summit crossing memorable.

In Whitehorse, the Taku Hotel staff was helpful and generous, and Alice Barton, formerly of Tourism Yukon, made many arrangements for my trip over Chilkoot and down the Yukon River. Atlas Tours of Whitehorse generously provided bus transportation from Whitehorse to White Pass. The staff at the Yukon Archives was very helpful, as were the Kanoe People (Scott Mcdougall and Brent Scott).

In Dawson City, the Klondike Visitors Association staff was gracious and helpful, as was the staff of the Downtown Hotel. It is always a pleasure to travel on the river with Captain Dick Stevenson, one of the constants in the changing Klondike.

In Seattle, Hilda Cullen and Robert Brown of the Canadian Consulate's tourism branch were instrumental in making this book possible, and in San Francisco Jill Matausek of the public relations firm of Rodin and Shelly Associates made many of my arrangements in Skagway. Juli Chase of Holland America–Westours helped with the Inside Passage material by arranging for me to travel several years ago from Vancouver to Juneau on the *Nieu Amsterdam* and between Juneau and Skagway on the *M/V Fairweather.*

Others who have been helpful over the years include James A. "Rocky" Richardson, former regional chief of interpretation for the National Park Service, Pacific Northwest; the late Mel Anderson, who kept the Klondike Festival on track when the seventy-fifth anniversary of the gold rush was celebrated in 1972; Ralph Munro, Secretary of State of Washington, who arranged for one of my many trips down the river; Alaska Airlines for assistance in the past; Skip Burns for introducing me to the Klondike; and Philip Mattera of the National Writers Union for his role in making it possible for this book to be published.

Prologue

It was a scene only a Dante of the North could have invented; more than twenty thousand men, women and children in the midst of winter blizzards trudging over a mountain pass in the Far North. They holed up in flimsy tents during blizzards. They were victimized by thieves and murderers and cheated by unscrupulous merchants. They suffered from frostbite, epidemics of spinal meningitis, influenza and food poisoning. They were buried by avalanches and flash floods. Yet back and forth they marched, day after day, week after week, like characters from Greek mythology cursed to spending eternity on the mountain pass.

This scene actually occurred during the winter of 1897–1898 at the height of the Klondike Gold Rush, when life was so difficult in North America that spending the winter in this manner seemed like a great opportunity. This dramatic scene has etched itself in the history of North America and has come to represent all gold rushes, even though the Klondike was the last to sweep the world.

This is the story of that great stampede and the park that commemorates it.

I became possessed with an irresistible longing to go to that land of romance and adventure.

—*Robert Campbell*
Hudson's Bay Company factor and founder of Fort Selkirk

Klondike Park

PART I | Yesterday

The First Europeans

The Klondike Gold Rush didn't just happen. It took decades for prospectors from all over North America to find the gold they *knew* was there. These true believers shambled into the Yukon from the Canadian Rockies, the American West, New Zealand, South Africa, South America, and Scandinavia. These were the men who would go to the ends of the earth in search of gold or whatever other precious ore they could find. To many of them the search was the thing, and the discovery was almost anticlimatic; how else can we explain how rapidly so many disposed of their fortunes and went back to the wilderness?

Before these searchers made their appearance, there were the Russians and Europeans, who had been trickling into the Yukon River drainage system for nearly two hundred years before the big gold strike of 1896. Ironically, although each nation was in search of something different, neither was officially looking for minerals. The Russians, led by the Danish seaman Vitus Bering on expeditions in 1728 and 1741, came in search of the land bridge connecting Asia with North America, a legend that still lived on in the oral tradition of the Siberian Eskimos. The English were looking for the Northwest Passage between Europe and Asia. The Spanish and Portuguese made token appearances but were not a factor in the drama that would eventually unfold.

The Russians obviously didn't find the land bridge. The English found a water route across the top of the continent, but the Northwest Passage was as useless then as it is now, impassable because of the Arctic ice pack.

Both nations did find something worthwhile: fur. From the natives they acquired fur from bear, wolf, fox, deer, raccoons, polecats and martens. Most important, they found millions of sea otter, which has the softest and most beautiful of all fur. Otter became to the North what beaver had been to the United States and southern Canada. In exchange for this most valuable of animal skins, the Europeans introduced metals to the Native Americans. Most of them immediately turned these metals into weapons, and their hunger for it was immediate and insatiable. In exchange for the furs, they accepted anything made of metal—brass buttons, copper kettles, tin canisters, spikes and belt buckles—and its ownership made them wealthy and powerful. The Europeans traders became more wealthy than they had imagined possible; it is doubtful that anything other than the gold the Spanish found from Mexico to Peru created more European wealth. The European traders were so greedy that they killed the otter to the edge of extinction and so ruthless in their treatment of native peoples that they took them as slaves and casually massacred them. Fortunately for the Inuit and interior Indians, the Russians limited their exploration and exploitation to the coast, from the Bering Sea to California, and briefly the island of Kauai. Thus, the Aleuts, who lived on the Aleutian Island and Alaska Peninsula, and the Sugpiaq, Eyak and Tlingits of the Alaska Peninsula and Gulf of Alaska bore the brunt of the Russian invasion.

Meanwhile, the English worked their way overland across Canada, establishing Hudson's Bay Company posts, one after the other, all the way from the St. Lawrence to the Mackenzie River drainage, then across the Rockies and north into the Yukon River system, each post serving the dual purpose of a place to trade for furs and a supply depot for the westward expansion of the company. When a new post was established on the edge of the frontier, it was stocked with food and supplies to be used by the next exploration party heading west, much the same technique Klondike stampeders would use as they established a series of caches for their food and equipment while struggling over Chilkoot and White passes.

Gold along the Yukon River was reported at various times by Hudson's Bay Company employees and their counterparts in the Russian American Company. Neither company wanted to hear about it. They were there for fur; they were fighting for control of the northern half of the vast continent and they knew that if the news of gold returned to civilization, their power would be diluted by the influx of American miners. A story persists that when Alexander Baranof, the Russian American Company leader, heard an employee talking about a gold discovery, Baranof ordered him shot.

The news inevitably leaked out; one version blames a Church of England minister for writing home about finding large nuggets in a stream. It is doubtful he can be blamed for everything. A more likely explanation is that he was one of many who mentioned gold in letters home and on street corners in Vancouver, Victoria and Seattle when prospectors went to these areas for a breather.

The prospectors began appearing in the 1850s along the North Pacific Coast, from Vancouver Island north. The mid–nineteenth century gold rushes in Colorado, Arizona, Nevada and California brought thousands of prospectors as far west as they could go. From the California coast those solitary souls who preferred life beyond the edge of civilization could go only south into Latin America or into the hostile north. A few headed south into Mexico and on into South America. Some who wandered north found gold along the Oregon coast and in the Cascade Mountains. A few modest discoveries were made in Washington and larger discoveries were made in the Idaho Panhandle. Few of these discoveries were large enough to create the millionaires of Arizona and California.

The prospectors edged farther north along British Columbia's Fraser River, where they found gold in 1858, and still farther north into the Cariboo Country of British Columbia, where the Barkerville discovery occupied their attention in 1859. They went up the Inside Passage by coastal steamer to Wrangell in Alaska and poled up the Stikine River through the coastal mountains into Canada and the headwaters of the Yukon River system. They went overland north from Vancouver. They paddled their boats up the Mackenzie River into the Arctic, hiking over a low divide and letting the Porcupine River carry them down to the Yukon. They went by ship from San Francisco, Portland, Seattle, Victoria and Vancouver to St. Michael Island off the mouth of the Yukon River in the Bering Sea, then paddled more than two thousand miles up the broad river, stopping to test every stream entering the Yukon.

All along the Yukon they found "colors," faint traces of gold, seldom enough to make it worthwhile to stop and winter over. This search for the mother lode went on for decades, and gradually, over a period of nearly fifty years, the number of miners grew from perhaps a score in 1850 to several thousand in 1895.

During this period the Americans hardly bothered to strengthen their hold on the Territory of Alaska. The place was so remote, and the government had been so harshly criticized by members of Congress and most of the American press for buying it in the first place, that it was virtually neglected. The only attempt to police it came from a small detachment of soldiers and the U.S.S. *Jamestown,* commanded by the resourceful Captain L. A. Beardslee.

The Hudson's Bay Company was also solidifying the English hold on the region east of Alaska and had numerous trading posts established long before the Alaska purchase. The English entry into the region was accomplished by building Lower Post on the Liard River and another post at Frances Lake, both near the continental divide, where the water begins flowing north rather than south. Next came the most remote of the posts, almost on the shores of the Arctic Ocean at Peel River. Lapierre House was built way up north beyond the Arctic Circle on the Rat River, and Rampart House was built on the Porcupine River. Then the traders built Pelly Banks on the upper Pelly River, followed by Fort Selkirk, a major post where the Pelly enters the Yukon River and the only post to survive to the present. Farther downstream was Fort Reliance near the Klondike River, and Fort Yukon was established where the Porcupine River enters the Yukon. With these in place, Hudson's Bay staked a claim to everything inland, while the Americans controlled almost all entrances from the Pacific Ocean.

One major roadblock to the interior of the North remained. The only practical route from the Inside Passage to the headwaters of the Yukon was via the Taiya River at the far northern end of the Inside Passage at the tip of the fjordlike Lynn Canal, which runs due north from Juneau. South along the mountain range lie the ice fields of the Coast Range, with no entry for hundreds of miles. North of Lynn Canal was the same; Glacier Bay and hundreds of miles of impassable mountains.

But there was one entrance at the head of Lynn Canal. The small Taiya River led the way to a low gap in the mountains that native Americans had been using for centuries. This gateway into the upper river was controlled by the Chilkats, a band of Tlingits who jealously guarded the route because they used it for trading with the interior tribes—the Sticks and Tagish along the headwater lakes, the Tutchones on the middle river and the Han tribes six hundred miles north.

The Chilkats were classic, ruthless middlemen. They treated the interior tribes with contempt and frequently made murderous raids to keep them subjugated. It was they who in 1852 taught the Hudson's Bay Company a lesson for competing with them: They burned Fort Selkirk to the ground and sent Robert Campbell and his employees paddling frantically down the Yukon.

The natives who lived in the Klondike area were members of the Athapaskans, who ranged from the subarctic all the way south to New Mexico. This small group was called the Han, meaning they were of the river. Unlike the coastal Tlingits, who had a wealth of food the year around without having to migrate for it, the Han had no choice but to be migratory. They lived along the Yukon River during the summer months, trapping and drying salmon. When autumn came, they moved away from the river to hunt moose and caribou for winter meat and skins for clothing and shelter. They supplemented their meat diets with berries, sometimes mashing it all together with dried fish or jerky.

Their life was as harsh as that of the Inuit and starvation winters were common. In these hard times they sometimes resorted to cannibalism in order to survive until spring. Yet they maintained a complex social system and religion that recognized reincarnation and several taboos involving food: they did not eat dog, wolf, raven, hawk or eagle.

As elsewhere in the Americas, the first native contact with Europeans was disastrous. Whole bands died from new diseases, and the Europeans' arrival completely changed the way the Han lived, making them dependent on the Europeans for everything.

When the gold rush occurred, a band of Hans were using the island at the mouth of the Klondike River as a fishing camp, but they were forced out by the stampeders. Some were able to sell their property, but most were simply shoved aside and ignored. They next moved to Dawson City, but the place they chose had already been selected by the North West Mounted Police as a site for their police post, so they moved three miles down the river to a year-around creek and established what became known as Moosehide Village, in part because that was the predominant building material for the Han dwellings, but also because the large slide scar on the mountainside between their village and Dawson City was called the moosehide. Finally in 1902 the 160-acre site was designated as an Indian Reserve and established its own school while the Anglicans built a church. Gradually, Moosehide was abandoned as the Han moved into Dawson City and other communities. By 1957, so few students were using the school that the territorial government withdrew funding for it.

During the pre–gold rush years, nobody had challenged the Chilkats' control of Chilkoot Pass and the interior Indians. But in the mid-1860s a mysterious man named George Holt and two native companions somehow slipped past the Chilkats. They hiked over the pass

Chilkoot Jack was the chief of the Chilkat band who led the first white men over Chilkoot Pass. Photo courtesy Yukon Archives.

to the headwater lakes and went on downriver, coming back the same way at the end of the summer and disappearing from history. Their crossing created the demand for access to this shortcut to the Yukon River, and the task of negotiating a treaty with the Chilkats fell to Captain Beardslee, the senior American military officer in Sitka.

In 1880, through a series of misadventures involving the making, drinking and selling of the noxious liquor called hooch, Beardslee was able to enlist Sitka Jack, the most powerful of the chiefs, to his side of the bargaining table. Beardslee had been permitting only certain tribes to make hooch, an agreement which required them to buy molasses and the stills from the whites for its production. Due to a dispute between the coastal tribes, Beardslee was able to trade rights to Chilkoot Pass for rights to manufacture the alcoholic beverage. Like so many treaties and agreements between the newcomers and natives, the result was lopsided in favor of the newcomers. Although the Chilkats could earn more money as packers, they lost their dominance and soon became bit players in the Klondike story. Undoubtedly the interior tribes were relieved to be rid of the Chilkats and their infrequent raids, but they, too, were relegated to insignificant roles.

This historic change was made official when in May 1880, Beardslee and his crew escorted nineteen prospectors from their winter quarters at Sitka to the mouth of the Taiya River, where they hired several Chilkats as packers to help them over the pass. This proved to the Chilkats that they would become richer packing miners' equipment than they could ever hope for trading with the interior tribes, so they assured Beardslee that access to the pass would be allowed provided the Chilkats held the packing concession. The agreement was the single most important factor in developing the Yukon River. It was the equivalent of the opening of the Panama Canal.

Meanwhile, the other main route, up the Yukon River from the Bering Sea, was being used by more and more prospectors coming into the region by way of paddlewheelers and various other kinds of boats from St. Michael. The first steamboat on the river belonged to the legendary Edward L. Scheiffelin, who discovered the Lucky Cuss Gold-mine in Tombstone, Arizona. Scheiffelin believed he could make an even greater discovery in the Yukon because he had a theory that an enormous band of gold encircled the globe from north to south. He put some of his newfound wealth where his beliefs were and bought a little paddlewheeler in San Francisco, naming it the *New Racket*, a curiously appropriate name because it was the first steamboat whose engine and whistle would be heard on the Yukon. He loaded it onto a schooner he chartered in San Francisco and struck out for the mouth of the Yukon River at St. Michael.

Scheiffelin and his crew sat out the winter of 1882–1883 locked in the ice of the Tanana River not far from its confluence with the Yukon, then continued up the Yukon the following summer. They found colors all along the route but no major deposits. Scheiffelin spent a year in the Yukon before calling it quits and declaring that the vast wilderness did not have sufficient gold to make it worth the effort. He sold the *New Racket* to a trader named Leroy Napoleon "Jack" McQueston, one of the most determined of the traders who grubstaked prospectors year after year.

At that time McQueston had two partners named Arthur Harper and Al Mayo; shortly before the gold rush they were joined by a fourth named Joseph Ladue. By this time most of the miners worked out of Circle City, a surprisingly orderly town McQueston had founded and named because he thought it was on the Arctic Circle: Actually it was some distance south. The prospectors lived a hard life with starvation, disease and fatal accidents always close by.

11

The traders had supplies shipped in from the coast and sometimes the food that arrived required a strong stomach. For example, chicken eggs were almost impossible to obtain because chickens couldn't survive the winters, so seagull eggs were collected along the coast and floated in barrels of seal oil for safe shipping up the river. The oil would be used for heating and lighting, but the eggs would be on the ragged edge of rotten, and those that were still fresh would usually taste of the rank seal oil. Thus, it is no surprise that once the Klondike stampede began, real chicken eggs and hens to lay them were one of the most valuable commodities in the region.

McQueston tried to grow potatoes and turnips, and even had a half-tame moose he hitched to a plow. The moose wasn't as agreeable or intelligent as horses and oxen, so McQueston hired men to pull the plow. The first crop of potatoes was killed by a late frost, but the turnips survived and were described as small but tasty by chroniclers of the town events. The next year he had a better crop because he planted on a hillside that faced south to catch more of the sun's warmth.

Thus the believers stuck it out, winter after winter, going about their remote lives, spending almost equal amounts of time on the basic business of survival and looking for the Mother Lode. They knew it was nearby. They had to believe that or the whole exercise was a waste of their time.

CHAPTER 2

Opening the
Classic Route

As the 1890s approached, more and more new-comers were reaching the Yukon River via Chilkoot Pass. The Chilkats increasingly relied on packing goods over the pass for their income and let the interior tribes buy from the Hudson's Bay Company and other traders. The whole experience took on an international flavor in 1882 when the Geographical Society of Bremen, Germany, sent two brothers, Arthur and Aurel Krause, to study the Tlingits and map the region.

In 1883 an American exploration party led by Lieutenant Frederick Schwatka arrived in the region. The mention of his name still rankles many Canadians—with good reason. Schwatka led a U.S. Army expedition onto Canadian soil without bothering to ask the Canadian government for permission, then he proceeded to name everything in sight. To compound this slight, forever after he persisted in referring to the entire region as Alaska because the international boundary had not been determined. Also it is easy to assume from the attitude reflected in his writing that Schwatka believed if it didn't belong to the United States, it should.

The expedition had been opposed by nearly everyone in the American military establishment because administration of the Territory of Alaska had been recently switched from the Army to civilians. Both the General of the Army and the Secretary of War had disapproved of any further exploration by the Army, but Schwatka's commanding officer, Brigadier General Nelson A. Miles, at Vancouver Barracks across the Columbia River from Portland didn't agree with them. He thought it was a mistake to take the military out of Alaska's administration, and he believed the place should be explored. Through some bureaucratic sleight of hand that involved renaming one or two programs to be funded, Miles found a way to produce funds for the trip, and he knew Schwatka was just the man for the job.

Schwatka was an arrogant and dapper man. He was the kind of man who didn't hesitate to boast of his abilities, and he was also the kind of man who wouldn't boast unless he could back it up. He had recently set an endurance record for the longest sled journey, being away from his base of supplies eleven months and twenty days. He had also led one of the many searches for the Franklin Expedition that was lost in the Arctic. Consequently, few Americans knew more about the Arctic wilderness.

Schwatka was given five Army men—a surgeon, a topographer–photographer, an artist and a storekeeper and his assistant—as well as a civilian guide. They quietly shipped out of Fort Vancouver aboard the coastal steamer *Victoria,* on May 22, 1883, bound for the head of Lynn Canal so they could go over Chilkoot Pass and build a raft to float all the way down the Yukon.

Schwatka's marching orders, apparently issued under the mistaken assumption that he would be on American soil, were for him to ascertain the number, character and disposition of the natives; their relations with each other; their feelings toward the Russian government and their attitude toward the United States. He was to study their way of life, how they communicated between regions, and types of weapons they used. He was also ordered to study the terrain, the best way to employ a military force in the region, the kinds of grasses for horse forage and the severity of winters.

His description of hiking over Chilkoot Pass with the band of Indian packers, building a raft and going down the lakes and the river is one of the most vivid of the pre–gold rush chronicles. His reports and subsequent book made it clear that his interests lay more in exploration and adventure than in the ethnological and anthropological material he was supposed to gather.

Eleven days after leaving Portland the steamer dropped anchor on the west side of Lynn Canal at Pyramid Harbor in Chilkat Inlet, where two salmon canneries had just been completed at the site of modern-day Haines. Schwatka proved his considerable negotiating skills when he managed to hire a band of packers in spite of the tribe being in mourning for the death of a major chief. After hiring about sixty packers, Schwatka then hired the cannery manager to use his powered launch as a tug to tow the canoes fifteen miles across the inlet to the mouth of the Taiya River. Schwatka wrote:

With a score of canoes towing behind, the ropes from the launch kept parting so often that we were considerable delayed, and as the Indians were seldom in a great hurry about repairing the damages, and treated it in a most hilarious manner as something of a joke on the launch, the master of that craft, when the rope had parted near the central canoe for about the twentieth time, finally bore on without them, leaving the delinquents to get along as best they could, there being about five more miles to make.

Then Schwatka in one sentence recognized the Chilkats' ingenuity and at the same time categorized that ingenuity as a form of laziness.

Fortunately just then a fair southern breeze sprang up, so that most of the tardy canoes soon displayed canvas, and those that could not hastily improvised a blanket, a pea-jacket, or even a broad-shouldered pair of pantaloons, to aid their progress, for the Indian in all sections of the country is much more ingenious than one is apt to suppose, especially if his object be to save manual labor.

The camp was about a mile upstream from the broad mudflat where the Taiya River enters Lynn Canal, and there the group found a group of interior, or Stick, Indians whom only recently the Chilkats had permitted to cross into their territory, further evidence that the old restrictions on Chilkoot travel were being removed. They were hunting black bear, which were abundant on the western slopes of the Coast Range. Although Schwatka was a determined and skilled negotiator, he was not a diplomat. He angered the Chilkats by hiring some of the Sticks as packers and paying them the same amount as the Chilkats, who had always considered the Sticks no better than slaves. Making the insult even worse, Schwatka hired a particularly strong Stick at half rates to go along as a spare in case one of the other packers fell ill. This Stick's primary job was carrying the military guidon, but he created another position for himself, that of ferrying the white men at the numerous fords across the Taiya River, earning a nickel each time he carried one of the men across.

Since it was mid-summer, daylight lasted more than twenty hours and it never became completely dark, so after establishing camp that night the packs, which weighed from 36 pounds to 137 pounds, were distributed among the Chilkats. For the first several miles the packers used their canoes to haul the equipment, towing them along with one man pulling while the other used a pole to keep the canoe clear of the bank and boulders. This ended seven miles up the swift river where the first cataracts appeared, which was where the town of Canyon City would soon grow.

From this point on the packers really earned their pay, scrambling over fallen trees and boulders made slick by wet moss, slipping into knee-deep bogs and wading through gigantic devil's club that stung like hornets and left large welts.

On the fifth day of the hike the Chilkats saw a mountain goat high in the mountains along the western wall, and in spite of the hard day's labor, one took off after it with an smooth-bore Hudson's Bay Company musket. The Chilkat managed to get above the goat and was descending toward him when a "little black cur dog" appeared just in time to frighten the goat, which started running straight at the camp. Men grabbed guns and began shooting but the terrified animal escaped unscathed.

On the sixth day they began the ascent of Chilkoot Pass, which made a deep impression on Schwatka.

> On the morning of the next day about five o'clock we commenced the toilsome ascent of this coast range pass, and by seven o'clock all my long back train was strung up the precipitous pass, making one of the prettiest Alpine sights that I have ever witnessed, and as seen from a distance strangely resembling a row of bowlders [sic] projecting from the snow. Up banks almost perpendicular they scrambled on their hands and knees, helping themselves by every projecting rock and clump of juniper and dwarf spruce, not even refusing to use their teeth on them at the worst places. Along the steep snow banks and the icy fronts of glaciers steps were cut with knives, while rough alpenstocks from the valley helped them to maintain their footing. In some such places the incline was so steep that those having boxes on their backs cut scratches in the icy crust with the corners as they passed along, and often-times it was possible to steady oneself by the open palm of the hand resting against the snow. In some of these places a single misstep, or the caving in of a foot-hold would have sent the unfortunate traveler many hundred feet headlong to certain destruction. Yet not the slightest accident happened, and about ten o'clock, almost exhausted, we stood on the top of the pass, enveloped in a cold drifting fog, 4,240 feet above the level of the sea. How these small Indians, not apparently averaging over one hundred and forty pounds in weight, could carry one hundred pounds up such a precipitous mountain of ice and snow, seems marvelous beyond measure. One man carried one hundred and thirty-seven pounds, while boys of twelve to fourteen carried from fifty to seventy pounds. I called this the Perrier Pass after Colonel J. Perrier of the French Geographical Society.

Once on top of the Pass the trail leads northward and the descent is very rapid for a few hundred yards to a lake [Crater Lake] of about a hundred acres in extent, which was yet frozen over and the ice covered with snow.

Later the same day they arrived at Lake Lindeman, where the packers dropped their loads for the last time. They had reached the head of navigation for the Yukon River. The packers were paid $10 to $12 each. To Schwatka's amazement, as soon as they were paid, they turned and began walking back up the trail, planning to make the entire twenty-five-mile trip to Lynn Canal without stopping.

Schwatka was on a nomenclature binge and labeled virtually everything in sight. He named glaciers they saw on the mountainsides along the route, but Perrier Pass itself refused to stick because Chilkoot was too well established. However, the lake they camped at retained the name he gave it in honor of Dr. Lindeman, secretary of the Bremen Geographical Society.

The earliest prospectors had already named the next lake Boat Lake for the simple reason that most built their boats here rather than taking a chance on running the river between the lakes. Schwatka renamed it in honor of James Gordon Bennett of the New York *Herald* because Bennett had underwritten expeditions all over the world, including sending Stanley to Africa in search of Livingston.

The party spent several days on the Lindeman shore building a large raft of "stunted spruce and contorted pine." They cut the trees along the trail above Lake Lindeman and floated them down the swift, boulder-filled stream into the lake. They lashed the logs together with the rope that had been used by the packers and they used an auger to drill holes through the logs into which long wooden pins, or dowels, were driven. The logs were also notched, or "saddled out" like corners of log cabins. On top of this they built a deck of pine poles elevated high enough to keep their provisions clear of most waves. A mast was added and a wall tent served as a sail. They also rigged a bow and stern oar for steering.

On June 16, 1883, the raft, which had been dubbed the *Resolute,* was launched and three of the men maneuvered it down the lake while the others walked along the shore. It successfully ran the rapids of the mile-long river connecting Lindeman and Bennett lakes, and they spent three more days on the shores of the Lake Bennett adding larger logs to the raft until it was forty-two feet long and sixteen feet wide. They also added two side oars for more propulsion on the lakes and control on the river. They launched it on June

Entering Lake Bennett from Lake Linderman

A recently built scow drifts down the rocky river from Lake Lindeman to Lake Bannett, circa 1898. Photo courtesy Yukon Archives.

19. Although they initially had a following wind to push them along, they were almost immediately hit by one of the gales common on the headwater lakes and nearly crashed onto boulders before they found shelter in a small cove. Fortuitously, in the cove were the largest logs they had yet seen, and they added four of them to the raft as stiffeners, making it much heavier but more seaworthy than before.

It took them two days to go the length of the thirty-mile-long lake and enter the two-mile river that drains Lake Bennett eastward into Nares Lake, which is actually part of the much larger Tagish Lake. Here at the small and slow Nares River was a place known as Caribou Crossing, where herds of woodland caribou crossed on their annual migrations. The local Stick tribe trapped the caribou while they were in the river, and a town later grew at the site. The original name of Caribou Crossing was used, but history gives Anglican Bishop William Carpenter Bompas credit for shortening it to its present name, Carcross, because he was given to abbreviating words in his letters home.

Schwatka remained consistent in his practice of naming everything. He named streams entering Lake Bennett the Wheaton River for Brevet Major-General Frank Wheaton, military commander in Alaska; the Watson River for Professor Sereno Watson of Harvard and the little

Nares River for George Strong Nares, a British explorer in the Arctic. Another of his names that didn't stick was Bove Lake, which appears on maps as Taku Arm. This lake, which runs some sixty miles due south into the heart of the Coast Range, narrows on its north end into a small stream that empties into a broad, relatively featureless lake the miners had called Mud Lake. Schwatka named it Marsh Lake, not as a commentary on its swampy shores but to honor Professor O. C. Marsh, an American scientist at the time. A river flowing into Marsh Lake near its outlet was named the McClintock River after Vice-Admiral Sir Leopold McClintock of the Royal Navy. It was McClintock who finally solved the mystery of the doomed Franklin expedition. Schwatka also named a peak on the eastern horizon Mount Michie for a West Point professor.

On June 29, just a few days over a month since they left Vancouver Barracks, their raft was caught in the current of the main Yukon River for the first time. Now they had to concern themselves only with steering. All of the local people they had encountered warned them of the narrow canyon ahead, and Schwatka had the impression it was only about five miles from Marsh Lake when in fact it is nearly fifty.

This stretch of the river can lull boaters into a false sense of security because it flows so smoothly and gracefully around gentle bends and through quiet forests. Then suddenly the canyon is just around a nondescript bend. Schwatka and his team were barely able to urge the lumbering raft to shore and tie it up before the swift current caught it. They walked along the canyon walls, attacked by millions of mosquitoes, to scout the deafening rapids and were enormously impressed by what they saw. Schwatka named it Miles Canyon to honor his commanding officer at Vancouver Barracks, Brigadier General Nelson A. Miles.

> The walls of the [canyon] are perpendicular columns of basalt, not unlike a diminutive Fingal's cave in appearance, and nearly a mile in length, the center of this mile stretch being broken into a huge basin of about twice the usual width of the stream in the canon, and which is full of seething whirlpools and eddies where nothing but a fish could live for a minute.

> Through this narrow chute of corrugated rock the wild waters of the great river rush in a perfect mass of milk-like foam, with a reverberation that is audible for a considerable distance, the roar being intensified by the rocky walls which act like so many sounding boards.

> At the northern outlet of the [canyon], the rushing river spreads rapidly into its former width, but abates not a jot in its swiftness, and flows in a white and shallow sheet over reefs of bowlders [sic] and bars thickly studded with intertwining drifts of huge timber, ten times more dangerous for a boat or raft than the narrow [canyon] itself, although perhaps not so in appearance. This state of things continues for about four miles further when the river again contracts, hemmed in by low basaltic banks, and becomes even narrower than before ... making a veritable horseshoe of boiling cascades, not much wider than the length of our craft, and as high at the end as her mast. Through this funnel of foam the waves run three or four feet high, and this fact made matters very uninviting for navigation in any sort of craft.

The upper canyon is Miles Canyon and the lower series of rapids were named Whitehorse Rapids because the standing waves reminded early arrivals of a horse's mane. This stretch of river, the only really exciting place along its 2,000-plus mile length, has been changed by the hydroelectric dam built between Miles Canyon and Whitehorse Rapids. The canyon walls still stand but the river hardly moves through it, and the Whitehorse Rapids have been replaced by the dam's spillway. One characteristic of the river Schwatka failed to mention is that Miles Canyon is so narrow that the water was forced into a crest two or three feet high for most of the way through. To be safe, boats and rafts had to ride its crest to avoid the sheer walls. Just outside the canyon were twin eddies which created whirlpools almost as frightening as the one described in Edgar Allan Poe's famous short story.

They spent the next day preparing for the whitewater run, presumably unloading the more precious items to be packed along the shore, and on July 2 cast off for the frightening trip. Schwatka's account was vivid, and probably quite accurate:

> A moment's hesitation at the [canyon's] brink, and quick as a flash the whirling craft plunged into the foam, and before twenty yards were made had collided with the western wall of columnar rock with a shock as loud as a blast, tearing off the inner side log and throwing the outer one far into the stream. The raft swung round this as upon a hinge, just as if it had been a straw in a gale of wind, and again resumed its rapid career. In the whirlpool basin of the canyon the craft, for a brief second or so, seemed actually buried out of sight in the foam.

> I was most afraid of the four miles of shallow rapids below the
> [canyon], but the raft only received a dozen or a score of smart
> bumps that started a log here and there, but tore none of the
> structure, and nothing remained ahead of her but the cascades.
> These reached, in a few minutes the craft was caught by the bow by
> the first high wave in the funnel-like chute and lifted into the air
> until it stood almost at an angle of thirty degrees, when it went
> through the cascades like a charge of fixed bayonets, and almost as
> swiftly as a flash of light, burying its nose in the foam beyond as it
> subsided.

Miraculously the large raft emerged from the canyon and rapids
with only slight damage. They wrestled it to shore and spent three days
repairing it at the site of Whitehorse. Here Schwatka and the expedition
doctor, both enthusiastic fly fishermen, were able to catch their first fish of
the trip. On the Chilkoot Trail they had no luck at all with the Taiya River
trout, but the grayling of the Yukon River were not so suspicious of lures;
they caught them by the score. Schwatka said that during the three days
they caught between three hundred and four hundred, which probably
isn't an exaggeration because grayling are among the easiest North
American fish to catch, especially where clear streams enter the lakes of
the river. They are so numerous in many places that you can literally
select your catch. If one comes after your bait that isn't large enough, you
simply flick the fly or lure away from it and wait for a better one.

Although Canadians with justification resented Schwatka's expedition, when the federal government built the hydroelectric dam
between Miles Canyon and the city of Whitehorse, the lake was named
in his honor.

The repaired raft was reloaded and Schwatka's party pushed off on
July 6, soon passing the mouth of the Takhini River, which Schwatka
didn't bother renaming. He did name a nearby hill in honor of Professor
Ernst Haeckel of Jena, Germany, who coined the term *ecology*. To his
credit he didn't try to rename the lake they came to that day. The natives
called it Kluk-Tas-Si, and Schwatka noted that it might have been Lake
Laberge of which he had heard. He was correct. The lake had been
named for Mike Laberge, a member of the exploration party for the
Collins telegraph line that was intended to go across Canada and Alaska
to Siberia, then down into Europe. The plan died when the first trans-
Atlantic cable was successfully laid, but not before the crews had cleared
thousands of miles of right-of-way through Canada. Oddly, Laberge

21

never got to see the lake but had spoken often and wistfully about its imagined beauty.

Schwatka couldn't help himself: He named the large island in the center of the lake for Freiherr von Richtofen, a prominent German geographer from Leipzig.

The lake is the last in the headwater system and one of the most difficult to navigate due to the sudden storms that come in from both the Arctic and the coast. Schwatka's experience on it is typical:

> At 1:30 P.M. a favorable breeze from the south sprang up, and by 2 o'clock was a raging gale, blowing over the tent where we were eating our midday meal, filling the coffee and eatables with sand and gravel, and causing a general scampering and chasing after the lighter articles of our equipment, which took flight in the furious wind. Most exasperating of all, it quickly determined us to break camp, and in less than half an hour we had all our effects stored on the vessel, and were pulling off the beach, when just as our sail was spread the wind died down to a zephyr hardly sufficient to keep away the mosquitoes. At 7 o'clock the lake was as quiet as can be imagined, and after remaining almost motionless for another hour we pulled into the steep bank, made our beds on the slanting declivity at a place where it was impossible to pitch a tent, and went to sleep only to be awakened at night by showers of rain falling on our upturned faces.

It took them three days to go the thirty miles down the lake and when they again felt the current of the river at the outlet, Schwatka wrote:

> I doubt if the besiegers of a fortress ever saw its flag go down with more satisfaction than we saw the rude wall-tent sail come down forever, and left behind us the most tedious and uncertain method of navigation that an explorer was ever called upon to attempt—a clumsy raft on a motionless lake, at the sport of variable winds.

The river that drains Lake Laberge is still known as the Thirtymile River because that is the distance from the north end of Lake Laberge to the river's confluence with the Teslin River. This is one of the most beautiful stretches of the Yukon, but Schwatka and his group were so busy struggling to control the raft that they hardly had time to appreciate the swift stream that winds its way between steep cliffs, small islands and around graceful turns. They made the trip down the Thirtymile River safely and one of their few complaints on the rest of the trip was their inability to always find a good place to camp with a breeze to keep mosquitoes away.

Schwatka named one river after Baron Adolph Nordenskiold, a Swedish Arctic explorer, and a short distance downstream they came to the only remaining rapids on the river, Five Finger and Rink rapids. They stopped to scout Five Finger Rapids, which he did not try to name. They chose the extreme right passage, which is the one nearly all boaters use. Schwatka correctly predicted that steamboats could use the same passage by installing a permanent cable so steamboats could winch themselves through the gap between the cliff on the bank and the first flowerpot island. Parts of the cable installed for that purpose remained just above the rapids for several decades.

A short distance downstream is the second set of rapids, which he named for Dr. Henry Rink, a Danish authority on Greenland. These rapids presented more danger then than Five Finger Rapids but this danger was eased during the steamboat era when the largest of the underwater boulders were dynamited out. Only a line of ripples remains.

At the time of Schwatka's trip, and for many decades afterward, the Yukon River didn't officially begin until Fort Selkirk, where the Pelly River enters from the east. The river from Marsh Lake down to Fort Selkirk was called the Lewes River, named by Campbell to honor John Lee Lewes, the Chief Factor at Fort Halket on the Liard River. Schwatka was one of the several explorers who tried to determine which was larger, the Pelly or the Lewes, and he correctly concluded that the Lewes was dominant. Eventually, the Yukon designation was moved back to the outlet of Marsh Lake.

Fort Selkirk was established in 1848 by Robert Campbell of Hudson's Bay Company, the final link in his plan to have posts throughout the Yukon River system. It was described by almost every traveler as a pleasant place to live and work. The fort stood on a flat, grassy knoll overlooking the confluence of the two rivers. The original fort was built on a nearby island but it took only one spring flood to convince Campbell that he had chosen the wrong site. The new fort commanded a sweeping view of the region, including the palisade of almost black basalt across the river that begins up the Pelly River and runs for several miles down the Yukon before disappearing into a grassy hillside. The fort had ample food from the land; moose and woodland caribou were in abundance the year around, and fish were easily trapped in a nearby slough.

However, Campbell was there before the Chilkats had grown accustomed to white men, and certainly before they were in a mood to negotiate away their dominance over the inland tribes. They came down the river about once a year to intimidate the inland tribes. With the Hudson's Bay Company's arrival, they showed their displeasure by camping near the fort and getting drunk and abusive to the Hudson's Bay men and the local tribes.

On the morning of August 20, 1852, Campbell and three men were cutting the tall native grass to store for the post's milk cow, when they saw five rafts bearing down on the post with twenty-seven Chilkats aboard. The Chilkats came ashore armed with firearms, and three of Campbell's employees lost their nerve and fled into the timber behind the fort, leaving Campbell with two men to face down the Chilkats. Campbell's diplomacy kept them from attacking immediately. After Campbell retired for the night, the Chilkats harassed residents of the post by shouting and trying to break into the buildings through locked doors and barred windows. The next afternoon two hunters and their families returned to the post from a trip up the Pelly River, and before they could escape, the Chilkats waded out into the swift water, grabbed the boat and pulled it ashore. Two of Campbell's men took guns away from two Chilkats and the battle was on. Several of them immediately rushed Campbell, who must have been living a charmed life—two natives tried to shoot him but both their rifles misfired. So many Chilkats were trying to subdue Campbell that they got in each other's way and he was neither shot nor stabbed. They wrestled him to the river's edge, then released him. His employees were also taken to the river's edge and released. The Chilkats permitted them to get into boats and the refugees headed downstream to the next post at Fort Yukon with the smoke of Fort Selkirk towering behind them.

Campbell and his group arrived safely at Fort Yukon and he left almost immediately for Fort Simpson at the confluence of the Liard and Mackenzie rivers to get permission to reestablish his beloved Fort Selkirk. He walked the entire distance only to find that nobody there had the authority to grant his wish. So he struck out again, this time on snowshoes, to Fort Garry, now Winnipeg, Manitoba. When he arrived, he had hiked more than two thousand miles but had no luck here, either. So he strapped on his snowshoes again and went down to Minnesota and boarded a train east to Montreal, where Hudson's Bay Company headquarters were. After the company told him to forget about Fort Selkirk, Campbell drifted into bitter obscurity.

After Schwatka reached the ruins of Fort Selkirk, which was little more than ashes and scattered fireplace stones, he showed that he wasn't totally insensitive to the efforts of others and stopped naming things.

> Here we were on land familiar to the footsteps of white men who had made maps and charts, that rough and rude though they were, were still entitled to respect, and accordingly at this point I considered that my explorations had ceased, though my surveys continued to the mouth of the river.

On July 18, Schwatka commented on a prominent landmark just downstream from the mouth of a river he thought was called Deer Creek, a scar from a landslide that resembled "a gigantic moose-skin stretched out to dry." This became perhaps the most familiar landmark along the entire river because it was here that the stampeders would soon congregate and where the town of Dawson City would be built just downstream from the Klondike River, née Deer Creek.

The rest of Schwatka's voyage was anticlimactic for him and his crew. They stayed with the raft until they reached Nukluklayet on August 6, where they boarded a small schooner bound for Anvik. There they caught the Alaska Commercial Company's steamboat *Yukon* to St. Michael on August 30 and sailed for home on September 11 aboard the schooner *Leo*.

CHAPTER 3

Canadians Come
from the East

When looking back over the decade before the gold rush, it is tempting to interpret the whole endeavor as a progression of events that led inevitably to the discovery of gold. It isn't accurate but it isn't too far from the truth, either, because by the 1880s gold was the dominant subject in the Yukon River drainage. The fur trade that first brought the Hudson's Bay Company to the region became a marginal economic factor among the white residents, mostly a means for prospectors who didn't have a good claim to support themselves while searching for gold.

Not all events of the period were dramatic, but many factors were at work in the prediscovery period that would have an impact on the Yukon once the gold was discovered. A good example is the group of explorers sent there by the Canadian government.

While hundreds of Americans were wandering into the Yukon, only a few Canadians were coming into the region, in part because then, as now, there were many more Americans than Canadians. When it became apparent that the northwestern corner of Canada was going to be populated whether a gold discovery was made or not, the Canadian government decided it had better take steps to make its presence felt and to strengthen its claim to the region. To do so, it set out to explore, survey and map the region from east to west.

This was the Canadian version of what Americans called Manifest Destiny, the widely accepted justification for moving America's international boundaries from the Atlantic to the Pacific and as far north and south as possible. Some skeptical historians have said it was a way of blaming God for the sins America committed against the aboriginal cultures and its competitors: Mexicans, English, French and Spanish.

Canadians were cut off from most of the Pacific coast by America's purchase of Alaska from the Russians, so the Canadian government wanted to stake a firm claim on everything between Alaska and the Atlantic as a buffer against the American's apparently insatiable hunger for real estate.

This they accomplished in a manner almost the opposite of the American approach. Americans tended to go forth to conquer the wilderness and the Native Americans, sometimes by killing everything in sight, then eventually getting around to establishing a legal system. Canadians sent the North West Mounted Police out ahead of everyone else to set up town sites, to negotiate with the Native Americans and to set up fair, or at least acceptable methods of apportioning the land. When the area was declared safe by the Mounties, settlers were invited to move west.

Thus, before the gold rush the Canadian government attempted to establish the basics of civilization in the Yukon wilderness and to be sure a governmental apparatus would be present in the event of a big gold strike. Another way to make its presence felt was to send out exploration parties to map the blank spots on maps.

Chief among the explorers was George Mercer Dawson, the assistant director of the Geological Survey of Canada. Dawson, a humpbacked dwarf, was one of the Yukon's most tireless explorers, and his notebooks bulged with his scientific observations, measurements, interviews with prospectors and natives and his running commentary on the countryside.

Another important explorer was William Ogilvie, a brilliant surveyor who worked for Dawson. Ogilvie set out with a third surveyor named Richard George McConnell in 1887 to survey and map the entire region between the Mackenzie River and the Pacific Coast. McConnell was also charged with mapping the Liard River area, after which he would cross the continental divide to the Mackenzie River and follow it north on the established trade route to the Arctic, then down the Porcupine River to the Yukon. Because his route was not so well known or so important to the Klondike story, few students of the Klondike pay much attention to his accomplishments.

Ogilvie followed the classic route to the Klondike, from the head of Lynn Canal over Chilkoot Pass and down the chain of lakes to Fort Selkirk, where the Yukon River officially began in those days.

Dawson accompanied McConnell up the Stikine River to Telegraph Creek, then overland to Dease Lake, where McConnell continued east while Dawson followed Robert Campbell's route north to the Pelly River and down it to Fort Selkirk. Their observations, measurements and commentary on the countryside proved invaluable to the prospectors who would come later, and modern canoeists particularly are indebted to the three geographers for their careful observations.

Dawson in particular was instrumental in keeping the search for the big strike alive because he found traces of gold all through the area. On the Pelly River he reported:

> Small "colors" of gold may be found in almost any suitable locality along the river, and "heavy colors" in considerable number, were found by us as far up as the mouth of the Hoole River, in the bottom of a gravel-bed there resting on the basalt. The headwaters of the MacMillan and Ross, and those of the Pelly itself yet remain not prospected, as well as the very numerous tributary streams of these rivers, in some of which "coarse" gold may yet be found.

Once he reached Fort Selkirk, Dawson prepared to head back to Lynn Canal, a tough voyage upriver that he dreaded because the river was swift and much of the route was through canyons and along banks thick with brush that made it impossible to line the boats along from the bank; the men had no choice but to paddle much of the way in their heavily laden boats. Ogilvie arrived at Fort Selkirk while Dawson and his men were building a new boat more suitable for the upstream voyage. During the voyage home Dawson took every opportunity to interview prospectors, of whom he found many, and natives living in fishing camps along the river. His commentary on the upper river was quite similar to Schwatka's testimony three years earlier. The major change that had occurred during those years was the construction of a windlass for hauling boats through Miles Canyon. His warning on Whitehorse Rapids was succinct: "The White Horse Rapid is, however, much more dangerous [than Miles Canyon] and though some of the miners have run through it—generally accidentally—it should not be attempted."

While they had seen perhaps dozens of prospectors along their route, the population increase was most evident when they reached the south end of Lake Lindeman where Chilkoot Trail ended. There Dawson found several boats along the shore and since it was late in the year (mid-September) groups of miners were leaving to winter over in Southeast Alaska. Consequently, Dawson had to wait two days for the next group of packers to arrive.

At the tidewater end of the trail, John J. Healy had built a small trading post at a town he named Dyea, another version of the word Taiya. Dyea stuck as the name of the town but the river remained Taiya on all maps.

Ogilvie was delayed by his inability to find enough packers to haul more than seven tons of what he called "impedimenta" distributed into 120 packs. Ogilvie enlisted the help of the trader Healy, his assistant named George Dickson and the commander of the U.S. gunboat *Pinta*.

Ogilvie also met four men who would soon be written into all history books, a "squaw man" George Washington Carmack, his in-laws Skookum Jim and Tagish Charlie and a former steamboat captain William Moore.

> Carmick [sic] spoke both languages [Tagish and Chilkoot] in a limited way, and had considerable influence with the Sticks. I employed him to help me over the pass and through his influence got a good deal of assistance from his Indian friends. Skookum Jim and Tagish Charlie were both there, and packed for me. Skookum well earned his sobriquet of "Skookum" or "strong," for he carried one hundred and fifty-six (156) pounds of bacon over the pass for me in a single carry. This might be considered a heavy load anywhere on any roads, but over the stony moraine of a glacier, as the first half of the distance is, and then up a steep pass, climbing more than three thousand feet in six or seven miles ... certainly is a stiff test of strength and endurance.

The second man soon to become famous, William Moore, had come into the area in 1883 with Joe Ladue. Both men remained in Northwestern Canada, Ladue as a trader and sawmill operator along the Yukon River system, and Moore as a steamboat skipper on the Stikine River during the Cassiar Gold Rush in 1876. Moore and his three sons made a fortune during that gold rush, but lost it when the gold petered out and they stayed with their steamboating too long. Armed with considerable entrepreneurial skills, Moore, then sixty-five, was on the lookout for another opportunity for a quick fortune and had heard of an alternate route over the coast range a few miles south of Chilkoot by way of the Skagway (or Skaguay as it was then spelled) River canyon. The route was supposedly of lower elevation and without the steep summit climb, and it, too, emerged at Lake Bennett. Ogilvie gave Moore permission to explore this pass but Moore had trouble getting natives to go with him because the Chilkats didn't want to reveal its existence, perhaps because it would dilute their control, giving them two rather than only one route to police. Moore finally talked a Native American named Jim into accompanying him. Some believe it was Skookum Jim but the information is inconclusive. The pass was named for the Canadian Minister of the Interior, Sir Thomas White.

What Moore had heard was true: The pass was lower but it was nearly ten miles longer and its route much more tortuous than Chilkoot. It led through swamps, over muskeg and through narrow canyons with the river on one side and sheer rock walls on the other. Once the trail rose out of the rivers and canyons it wandered across a hostile boulder-and lake-strewn landscape that was so soggy that the boulders seemed to be islands. But Moore saw it as the source of his next fortune. In 1888, he built the first cabin in what would become Skagway preparing for the human flood he was certain would come.

As the traffic through Lynn Canal grew, Moore became more ambitious and built a thirty-by-sixty-foot wharf against the sheer bluff. A determined man, he would have to wait eight years for his dream to come true. He and his sons locked their cabin and moved down to Juneau, coming back to Skagway from time to time to check their cabin and wharf, which eventually rotted and collapsed.

More and more people came into the Yukon: surveyors for both the American and Canadian governments to establish the international boundary, sportsmen on a lark, prospectors in search of the mother lode, traders and other entrepreneurs, missionaries, anthropologists and finally the first policeman—a man of towering integrity and common sense named Inspector Charles Constantine, who arrived at the head of Lynn Canal on June 29, 1894, with Staff Sergeant Charles Brown. They were enroute to the settlement of Fortymile, where most of the prospectors were gathered, earning wages but still unable to find the big one.

Many places along the Yukon River were named for their distance from old Fort Reliance, the first major post along the river that was a short distance downstream from the Klondike River. Fortymile, which was downriver from Fort Reliance, became the major post and residential area for miners covering several thousand square miles both upstream and downstream.

Constantine's description of the village gives an insight to the conditions during a period when many miners had paying claims but none of gold-rush proportions.

The village or camp consists of about 150 log cabins, of an average size of 20x24 feet. There are about half a dozen fair sized houses, two or three being two stories high. McQuestion [LeRoy Napoleon "Jack" McQueston] and Company have a large warehouse. The flat on which the camp is built contains about 700 or 800 acres, and is divided from the mainland by a ravine which, during the period of high water, is a fair sized river.

He estimated the population at about 260 and said that many more were expected to live there the winter of 1895. He said the majority were Americans and Canadians with a scattering of Scandinavians, English-men, an Arab, three Armenians, one Greek and one Chilean. Yet the miners were definitely racist: When a group of Chinese and Japanese miners landed at Dyea, the miners had a meeting and voted to bar them from the Yukon.

The miners had established their own legal system through the occasional town meetings called to discuss a problem. Constantine reported that when two men got into a fight that involved a shooting and knifing, the miners met and told the men that they would be ordered out of the country if more trouble erupted, and if one killed the other, the killer would be hanged.

He said Fortymile was very quiet for a mining camp, and noted that "a woman is treated with more respect here by the miners than she would be in an eastern town by those who are supposed to be far above them, morally and socially."

Constantine's inventory of the various diggings showed that men on some creeks were panning up to $21 a day, that claims on the Stewart River were the best and that mining production in 1893 was about $300,000 while fur trapping yielded between $40,000 and $50,000.

The major player in Fortymile, "Jack" McQueston, was away during Constantine's visit. He was building a new town called Circle City; he thought it was on the Arctic Circle but actually was some distance south. A modest discovery had been made on Birch Creek, a stream that emptied into the Yukon, so McQueston hauled in some supplies from Fortymile and set up storekeeping.

In 1895, the yield from local mines was about $400,000. The big discovery still lay waiting in an obscure creek.

CHAPTER 4

The 1890s:
A Decade of Misery

The decade of the 1890s in the United States has always confounded historians and sociologists. On the one hand the period has been referred to as the Gay Nineties, while on the other it was notable for the terrible living conditions throughout much of the world. Some historians have gone so far as to say that the United States underwent a national psychic crisis during that period.

It may well be true. America suffered its worst economic depression after the Panic of 1893. The economic collapse came after a period of overexpansion by railroads and unchecked speculation on Wall Street. Foreign investors became frightened by the American calamity and sold off their American bonds. This drained gold from the American treasury at a time when political leaders were arguing over whether the nation should tie its treasury to gold or silver. This debate and the obsession with the metals was one more factor in the desperate search for gold.

The depression that followed was horrible, perhaps the worst the United States has yet suffered. The nation had no social programs for its citizens. It was running on capitalism at its most fundamental level; everyone for himself or herself, and the distance between the have's and have not's was vast. It is doubtful that America was ever in a more vulnerable position. Fortunately, it had no natural enemies at that time, and threat from without was almost nonexistent. Had it not been for the banker and businessman J. P. Morgan stepping forward and single-handedly bailing out the American government by underwriting the Treasury when it was almost drained, the entire monetary system could well have disintegrated.

The obsession with gold and silver made discoveries of both metals in Colorado, Arizona, California, British Columbia and other parts of the world particularly attractive to the poor, who had few other means of obtaining wealth.

The disastrous Panic of 1893 was not limited to the United States. All of North America was in trouble, and the United States took Europe, much of South America and South Africa with it to the edge of collapse. The Panic of 1893 also occurred at a time when Americans were already questioning their nation and their leaders. Effects of the Civil War were still visible in the South. The wounds, still with us nearly 150 years later, were open sores then, and carpetbaggers traveled the South creating moral and economic havoc.

The Western frontier was becoming less a dream of free, rich land and more a harsh reality of relentless work with little to look forward to but more work. In spite of the American promise of free land for all citizens willing to move west to claim it, life was too harsh for the promise of wealth and independence to be fulfilled. Railroad and steamboat companies had salesmen traveling the length and breadth of Europe and Russia seeking farmers and laborers to fill ships bound for New York. Cheap labor for railroads was being imported from China and Japan. The railroads had been given millions of acres in exchange for building lines across America, and they needed a supply of peasants to turn the prairies and plains into farms and ranches to fill their boxcars.

So the immigrants came to Ellis Island and the dingy quarantine shacks along the West Coast. They worked their way across the country, and those who had fled the poor land of Europe with its wars and rigid social classes, and the Orient with its feudal system and warlords, found themselves in a vast new land and deeply in debt to railroads and merchants. They were foreigners among other foreigners in a land that was home to none.

Across the Great Plains, church bells tolled the ages of people who just died. Newspapers routinely carried stories about people going insane and walking down streets nude, of young men being driven mad by college hazing, of accused murderers committing suicide by eating pieces of bed springs, of women shearing off their hair while walking in their sleep. When someone was committed to a hospital with an incurable disease, the paper would state matter-of-factly that the patient would die and it was seldom wrong.

Psychiatry was in its infancy—Freud was at work but was not yet a household name—and most of those who studied the human mind wrote of mental disorders in the moralistic and religious vernacular of the time. One social scientist named George Beard discovered a disease he named American nervousness and said Americans suffered from an insufficiency of nerve force, much like one of Edison's new electric lights that dimmed from a weak current. Beard blamed steam power, the press, the telegraph, science and the mental activity of women. Some city planners opposed tall buildings because elevators were dark and dank and breeding places for all manner of disease. Since so many things were wrong with the country, American citizenry tended to take such men seriously.

It was during this period that the first wave of landowners fled to the cities because it was not economical for so many families to live on farms. With the economy virtually at a standstill, newspapers were filled with stories of financial failures that spawned thousands of moving sales, suicides, and cases of madness that filled insane asylums to overflowing.

With so many people destitute and with so few options available, America became obsessed with gold, and the debate over gold versus silver created even more demand; prospecting for gold and silver became a national passion. The California Gold Rush of 1848–1849 firmly imprinted gold in the American psyche and the smaller discoveries that followed only served to whet the dream of instant wealth.

With these conditions being accepted as normal, it is easier to understand why people would soon feel fortunate to have the opportunity to willingly subject themselves to the agonies of the Klondike Gold Rush.

CHAPTER 5

August 16, 1896

By 1896, the Yukon was ready. All the characters in the drama were on stage; the rehearsals were over. Long before the gold rush some of the old-timers said they could feel it in the air, like an approaching prairie thunderstorm or an earthquake along the San Andreas Fault. They were positive it would come; they just didn't know where it would happen or when.

For most of those along the Yukon River in the summer of 1896 it was business as usual. The miners were so remote from the rest of the world that they hardly knew or cared what was going on elsewhere. Every year they were there, they would have no news of the world from October until June. Most didn't seem to care. They lived in an information vacuum and liked it. The economic depression and emotional upheaval it brought were of only slight interest. They were earning a living of sorts, they lived in a reasonably well structured society that they controlled themselves, and they were free to dream their dreams of vast wealth while tramping along the creeks and rivers looking for the bouquet of nuggets that would represent the mother lode. The wealth itself wasn't the primary goal for some of the most dedicated prospectors: It was the search and the discovery that interested them. The true prospector searches his entire life, and history has ample examples of prospectors who became wealthy but who preferred being out in the wilderness living off the land rather than building a mansion in San Francisco and wearing expensive clothes. Life in the wilderness was much more fundamental and based directly on survival, while in the cities many problems were manufactured by people with too much time on their hands and too few real things to worry about.

Usually when something extraordinary happens, the daily, mundane chain of events leading up to it becomes more heroic than the facts will support. That is not the case with the Klondike discovery. This event has always been tainted by bitterness, racism and broken promises, and the two Caucasian men involved could hardly be described as heroic. Unlike many momentous events, no elaborate mythology has grown around the Klondike discovery. The original version, which nearly everyone believes, has changed little in a century of telling. The story is neither a glamorous nor a joyful story.

The discovery was made on August 16, 1896, by the men who had helped Ogilvie over Chilkoot Pass a few years earlier: George Washington Carmack, who was more or less married to a Stick woman named Kate; her brother Tagish Charlie and another Stick named Skookum Jim. According to some accounts, Kate and their young daughter were with them on the discovery trip. That they were nearly six hundred miles from their traditional home at Caribou Crossing gives an idea of how far the natives traveled during the summer months.

The fourth member of the cast was Robert Henderson, a solitary prospector born and reared in New Brunswick who had a reputation of being fanatical about his quest for gold. Ogilvie wrote that "those who knew him best do not believe he would work the richest claim on earth if he had to stay on it till it was worked out." The man was a traveler and a searcher, the prototype of a prospector.

Henderson spent fourteen years prospecting in Colorado before moving north with two other men whom history has relegated to solo names, Kendrick and Snider. They crossed Chilkoot in 1894 and Henderson settled in the Yukon region, grubstaked by Joe Ladue from his trading post at the mouth of the Sixtymile River. Henderson prospected the Indian River through the winter of 1895–1896, and the following summer, while on his way back to Ladue's post, crossed over a divide and hiked down to a creek he hadn't worked before and found a considerable amount of gold. He worked the stream until July 1896, ran out of food and returned to Ladue's post. However, the season was dry and the streams low and his moosehide boat kept running aground, so he decided to return a different way that involved going up the river the natives called Trondiuck—meaning hammer-water because the natives hammered stakes into it as fish traps—then crossing over a divide back to the Indian River drainage.

Henderson packed his little boat over the ridge and down to the Trondiuck, then drifted down toward the Yukon. At the mouth of the river he found Carmack, Tagish Charlie, Skookum Jim and Kate camped there and he stopped to chat with them. Carmack told Henderson they were on a fishing trip and that they might also cut some logs and float them down to the sawmill at Fortymile.

Carmack had a reputation of laziness and a carelessness with the truth. Compared with most other white men in the North, he was indeed lazy, working only when necessary, and then not very hard, and traveling around the big empty country more from curiosity than ambition.

During their conversation, Henderson told Carmack and his group that he had found gold on what Henderson called Gold Creek, and Carmack said he and his companions would stake claims on it. Henderson, a racist, objected and said he didn't want natives on his creek. Carmack was angered, and on this note Henderson left for Sixtymile.

Henderson returned to Gold Bottom with his provisions and resumed work. In the meantime, the Carmack party continued fishing and discussed felling some trees to make the logs, so Skookum Jim went up the Trondiuck River to look for trees. He found some tall, straight ones on a creek that had been known as Rabbit Creek. He looked over the stream to see if it was deep enough to float the trees. As he did so, he found gold on the bottom. Lots of gold. He raced back to tell Carmack, who wasn't interested in gold at that moment. Some three weeks later he changed his mind and decided to hike up the stream and see if Jim was correct. Ogilvie tells what happened next:

> Jim, Charlie and George started up Bonanza [the stream was quickly renamed] on the quest with a gold pan, spade, axe, and such other tools as were necessary for a prolonged stay from camp, and such provisions as their means afforded, and according to the Indians the supply was not extensive or diversified, being mostly fish. Traveling up the valley of Bonanza through the thick underbrush at that season was tiring and fatiguing, and the mosquito-laden atmosphere added torment to fatigue. A short distance below where they afterwards made discovery, both Jim and Charlie told me they, while panning during a rest, found a ten-cent pan. ... It was decided that if the Gold Bottom trials failed they would devote attention to this place. The Indians both told me they asked George if they would tell Bob [Henderson] of this find, and that George directed them to say nothing about it till they came back, if they did, and investigated further, then if they found anything good they might tell.
>
> Traveling was so tiresome and tedious in the valley that, when they came to the confluence with the creek now called Eldorado, they

took to the divide between it and Bonanza, and followed the crest of this divide around the head of Bonanza Creek, where, finding the marks made by Henderson, they descended to him. Arrived there they were nearly bare of provisions, and completely out of tobacco, a serious predicament for Jim and Charlie. Henderson, either through shortage himself or dislike of the Indians, or both, would not let them have anything, though Jim and Charlie both assured me they offered to pay well for all they could get, which Jim was both able and willing to do. As they did not find any prospect approaching in value the ten-cent pan on Bonanza, they remained a very short time at Henderson's camp, and made their way back to the head of the creek which first gave fame to the Klondike—Bonanza.

They left Henderson, really angry at him this time, and went hunting for a moose because they were hungry. Jim shot one and shouted for the others to come to him. While waiting for them, he went down to the stream for a drink and when he looked at the bottom, he saw more gold than he had ever seen anywhere in his life. They cooked part of the moose, and after they had eaten, Jim showed Carmack and Charlie the gold. They spent two days panning and testing the creek for the best deposit, and on August 16, 1896, selected a spot to stake the discovery claim.

Skookum Jim rightfully believed he should have the discovery claim, which also entitled him to stake another claim adjoining it, giving the discoverer a total of 1,000 feet along the stream. Carmack disagreed and told Jim it would have to be registered in his name because natives would not be allowed to record a discovery claim. Carmack, Jim and Charlie argued into the night and finally Carmack relented enough to assign half interest in the discovery claim to Skookum Jim. The next day they staked the discovery claim.

No. 1 was the discovery claim. No. 1 below discovery went to Tagish Charlie while No. 1 above discovery went to Skookum Jim. Bob Henderson was not told of this and didn't learn of it until long after all the claims along Bonanza Creek had been staked. During this frenzy Henderson had been patiently working Gold Bottom Creek over the ridge. He lost out entirely. Even Gold Bottom Creek was staked below him by Andrew Hunker, who renamed it Hunker Creek. He only heard of the discovery by accident when he met two prospectors named George Wilson and James McNamee, who told him the news. One man referred to it as "the biggest thing in the world," and when they told him Carmack found it, Henderson threw down his shovel in disgust.

He remained in the Yukon most of his life, never finding a decent strike, eternally bitter toward Carmack for not telling him of the discovery and unrepentant for his racist attitudes. Toward the end of his life the Canadian government put him on a pension of $200 a month for life. He died in 1933 while planning a prospecting trip on the Pelly River.

CHAPTER 6

The Winter of Wealth

T he information vacuum of the Klondike was complete. Nobody as far south as Vancouver, Victoria or Seattle knew of the discovery until eleven months later. The news did work its way up and down the Yukon River via the "moccasin telegraph," and by October the first two stages of the three-stage stampede had already occurred.

The first stage consisted of prospectors already in the area who immediately filed claims. By the middle of September 1896, some two hundred claims had been filed on Bonanza Creek and its tributaries, and gold was also found along the Indian River across a low divide to the south and on Bear and Hunker Creeks up the Klondike River a short distance. This initial, local stampede turned established camps such as Fortymile and Circle City into immediate ghost towns as the miners deserted their claims and abandoned their cabins. Very few had been earning much more than enough to get through from season to season, and it was well worth taking their chances upriver at this new site.

The second stage occurred in early 1897 when the word reached other prospectors south in Alaska and on down the coast toward Vancouver and Seattle. Approximately 3,000 of these packed up and headed overland to the diggings. This might be called the insiders' rush because the information passed from prospector to prospector and few people outside this fraternity heard the news. Even if they did hear about the strike, everybody had heard similar stories many times before because no other profession relied more on enthusiasm and positive thinking than prospecting.

The third stage wouldn't occur until July 1897, when the first prospectors with gold in their pockets arrived in civilization and created the enormous gold rush.

Vern Gorst, who later founded an airline that became United Air Lines, worked a claim at 16 above Eldorado. Photo by Asahel Curtis.

During the fall and winter of 1896 the miners found more and more gold in the streams. They panned the surface, and then dug down through the various layers of the stream bed for the nuggets and dust that had accumulated over uncountable centuries. The Klondike River valley took on the look of a battlefield as trees were felled for sluice boxes, shacks and firewood to thaw the permafrost above the gold deposits. The valley filled with wood smoke as the gravel was laboriously thawed and piled in heaps.

Once the surface gravel was panned or sluiced, the miners next had to work their way down through the permafrost to bedrock, because in most claims the gold lay in three levels below the present stream beds. There was no average depth: That first winter they found the first layer as shallow as eight feet and as deep as thirty feet. In years to come the area would be worked as deep as three hundred feet.

Their worst enemy was the permafrost that began about a foot below the surface. They built fires and stoked them for several hours, then let them burn out and scooped out the thawed dirt, sand and gravel into piles near the sluice. Then they built another fire and repeated the procedure. Once they arrived at a layer of gold-bearing gravel, they had to follow it by "drifting," meaning they next thawed a horizontal shaft. This was a very unpleasant job because they constantly breathed the smoke that hung in the shafts. When spring came they had to be careful to avoid cave-ins when the dirt and gravel thawed. Water constantly dripped on them. The early summer months were best for mining because of the ample water supply for sluicing, but when summer waned, so did the water level in the streams, and the sluices slowly dried up with the approach of autumn.

All through the winter they chopped or sawed down trees, sawed them into manageable lengths, built fires and scooped the muck into piles, trying not to think too much about their riches. In the meantime, all the traders and sawmill owners in the Fortymile and Sixtymile areas moved their shops to a piece of flat land that Joe Ladue had platted just downriver from where the Trondiuck River, by now called the Klondike, empties into the Yukon. Ladue named his instant city in honor of the dwarf geologist George Mercer Dawson. Looming over this boomtown was an enormous scar on the mountainside left by a landslide hundreds of years earlier. The scar is the only distinguishing landmark for many miles along the river, and some superstitious prospectors wondered if the scar wasn't really a beacon nobody had heeded to lead them to the Klondike River. From a distance its tan color caused it to be called the moosehide by some prospectors, and that name was given to the Han village just downstream. About the only positive thing to be said about Dawson City's location was that the Klondike River created an eddy as it flowed into the Yukon and this made landings easier for the steamboats, rowboats, canoes, rafts and scows that came downstream.

When spring came at last in 1897 the cleanup began, and when the first steamboats came upriver the seventeen hundred miles from St. Michael, more than eighty prospectors were waiting for their first trip home in several years. All had come to the Yukon virtually destitute, and now they were leaving for home with so much gold they could hardly carry it aboard. Gold was in suitcases, jars, medicine bottles, boxes and bundled in clothing. They loaded more than three tons of gold aboard the small steamboat *Alice* and the larger *Portus B. Weare* and began the voyage back to the Bering Sea. There was so much gold aboard the two vessels that some of it was stored out on the open decks as casually as if it were firewood.

At St. Michael the miners boarded two coastal steamers. Several boarded the *Excelsior* bound for San Francisco, and sixty-eight bought tickets on the *Portland* bound for Seattle. The *Excelsior* made better time and landed in San Francisco two days before the *Portland* reached Puget Sound. The *Excelsior* caused very little stir in cosmopolitan, we've-seen-everything San Francisco. A crowd gathered when news of the scruffy miners' wealth was spread, and newspapers carried stories. Somehow the chemistry wasn't right. Perhaps it was the distance, nearly three thousand miles. Whatever the reason, nothing happened.

When the *Portland* arrived two days later in Puget Sound on July 17, 1897, the less world-weary Seattle was ready for it. A Seattle *Post-Intelligencer* reporter and a few others chartered a tug to go out and meet the ship after it cleared customs at Port Townsend. One of the *Post-Intelligencer's* best reporters, Beriah Brown, had the tug pull along side so he could climb aboard the ship while it was under way. He had a quick look around at gold nuggets stacked wherever there was room, interviewed some of the miners, climbed down the ladder to the tug and ordered the skipper to give it full throttle. When the editors saw his story, they quickly called for a special edition of the paper.

"Gold! Gold! Gold!" the paper screamed. "68 rich men on the steamer *Portland*. Stacks of yellow metal," said the banner headlines. Then Brown wrote a simple sentence that set North America on fire: "At 3 o'clock this morning the steamer *Portland* from St. Michael for Seattle, passed up the Sound with more than a ton of gold aboard."

It is probably the most electrifying lead sentence ever published in a Seattle newspaper, and certainly one of the greatest in American journalism. Its impact was immediate; the city and the entire North American continent was almost immediately changed.

The Klondike Gold Rush, the last of the great nineteenth century stampedes for gold, started before dark. Seattle went into an immediate frenzy. So many people were milling around on the streets that the streetcars couldn't nudge their way through the crowds. Some streetcars were simply abandoned by their conductors, who went home, packed and took off for the Klondike. People began selling everything to get a grubstake, and coffee cans filled with savings were unearthed from back yards. Several Seattle policemen resigned, most of Tacoma's fire department resigned and several stores had to close early because they had no clerks. All berths were soon taken for the passage north to St. Michael aboard the *Portland*.

On July 18, 1897, only one day after the *Portland* arrived with the sixty-eight haggard but very rich miners, the steamer *Al-Ki* departed north with stops scheduled for Juneau, Douglas, Wrangell, Skagway and Dyea. It was filled to the brim with passengers, 350 tons of miners supplies, nine hundred sheep, sixty-five head of bawling cattle and fifty horses. The ship was only 201 feet long with a beam of 22 feet and it is difficult to imagine how they managed to get everything loaded and underway in less than twenty-four hours after the gold rush began.

The frenzy spread across North America as the telegraph wires began buzzing with news stories about the strike and with telegrams sent to relatives and friends back east with pleas for money. One read, "A grubstake, for God's Sake."

One of the most famous victims of the Klondike madness was W. D. Wood, the mayor of Seattle, who was in San Francisco at the time. He telegraphed his resignation to the city council and chartered the steamship *Humboldt,* rounded up some passengers and on August 16 struck out for the mouth of the Yukon. His was not a happy crew. He set the tone of the voyage by trying to leave fifty-thousand pounds of his passengers' luggage on the dock. They were so angry and unruly by this time that several of them grabbed the ex-mayor and were trying to hang him at the dock when help arrived.

The passengers' desire for gold was stronger than their desire to see the last of Wood, so they struck out on the voyage and reached St. Michael on August 29. Only after all the passengers and cargo were off-loaded on the windy Bering Sea beaches did Wood tell them a minor detail he had somehow forgotten to mention earlier: "By the way, the steamboat that will take you upriver to the Klondike? You will have to build it yourself." At least Wood had thoughtfully brought along the makings of the sternwheeler, which accounted for his attempt to leave the passengers' luggage behind. With no choice but comply, the passengers pitched tents and set to work building the *Seattle No. 1,* which was completed in an amazing three weeks. It was a distinctly ugly craft and was forever named after the northern native footwear Mukluk because it was low and squat with no definite lines. The unhappy group was able to get only halfway up the river before the ungainly boat was frozen in for the winter with the Klondike River more than eight hundred miles away. They built a shantytown on the river bank and called it Suckerville. For fuel they helped themselves to Wood's precious hoard of lumber that he had brought along to sell in Dawson City. In the middle of the winter, Wood, who had somehow managed to avoid being lynched, sneaked out of Suckerville, headed downriver to St. Michael and fled home to blessed anonymity. The others stayed, and two couples were even married that winter. They arrived in Dawson City on June 25, 1898, nearly a year after leaving San Francisco.

Unfortunately, the Wood adventure was more or less typical of schemes to go north. Steamship companies and railroads worked together to fill seats and berths, and told the unsuspecting and desperate whatever came to mind in order to get them to buy tickets. Some groups were dropped off in the Yakutat area with directions to cross the Malaspina Glacier, the largest glacier in North America. Some managed to survive the trek but many others died.

Seattle quickly established itself as the gateway to the Klondike, largely through a well-orchestrated campaign by the advertising committee of the Seattle Chamber of Commerce. A former newspaperman, museum curator, politician and Paraguayan Consul Erastus Brainerd set out to corner the Klondike outfitting business for Seattle and succeeded. Obviously he had geography in his favor because Seattle was closer to Alaska and the Yukon than any city other than Vancouver, but Brainerd wanted to be sure inland cities didn't get the pleasure of selling prospectors clothing and tools before they got to Seattle.

He gave the committee the more official-sounding name of the Bureau of Information and talked the Washington Secretary of State into sending out letters over his signature. He had circulars printed that looked like official rather than promotional pieces, and coordinated the writing and printing of special newspaper sections filled with accurate information on how to prepare for the rigors of the Klondike. He had these special sections sent to every one of the seventy thousand postmasters in America with the request to display them. He bought larger ads than his competition—Tacoma, Vancouver, Victoria, Portland and San Francisco in particular—and had them placed in all the nation's major newspapers and magazines. He asked Seattle residents, most of whom were born elsewhere, to help by writing letters to their hometown newspapers telling of Seattle's advantages. When Seattle was treated negatively by a newspaper, Brainerd or someone with a powerful title would write a letter to the editor correcting the statement. Brainerd himself wrote dozens of features and sent them to newspapers and magazines everywhere. To his and the city's eternal credit, the information they sent out was accurate and painted no rosy pictures of the journey the Klondikers faced.

Before the real stampede began, the North West Mounted Police had established a minimum requirement of food and equipment for people entering the Yukon, with the main requirement being a year's supply of food. The threat of a famine hung heavy over the isolated region, and for decades after the gold rush storekeepers throughout the

Yukon were required by law to keep at least a year's supply of staples on their shelves. Brainerd got a copy of the equipment list, its approximate value, and had it published and posted everywhere:

> Outfit: One man, one year, including groceries, clothing, bedding, hardware, medicine chest and other necessary articles. An outfit costing less will be defective in what may be necessary to save life, and at that price food will be coarse, though it is all that very many take. In this estimate groceries are figured at about $60 for a year's supply ... .

He next listed the various routes to the gold fields, which included the "all water route" to St. Michael, then up the Yukon River. He didn't know then that only those who left Seattle early in the season could make the trip in one summer; otherwise, people had to sit out the winter. However, Brainerd estimated it would take between thirty and forty days to go from Seattle to Dawson City by this route.

The next alternative was the classic route: From Seattle up Lynn Canal to Skagway or Dyea, then hike over Chilkoot or White Pass to Lake Lindeman and Bennett, build a boat and go on down Tagish Lake and Lake Marsh into the river to Lake Laberge and on to Dawson City.

The third route was by ship to Juneau, then up the Taku River, which was no route at all. The fourth listed was across the Kenai Peninsula, also a nonroute. He didn't mention any of the overland routes through western Canada, which was humane, because they were among the worst routes tried. More practically, to do so could have diluted Seattle's share of the business.

Brainerd guessed the distances from Seattle to be 2,500 miles to St. Michael, and another 1,723 miles up the Yukon to Dawson City. The classic route was 1,500 miles: 834 miles by water to Skagway and Dyea, 29 miles overland from Dyea to Lake Lindeman, and 641 miles by lake and river from Lake Lindeman to Dawson City.

From Seattle to Skagway took seventy-two hours on a coastal steamer, and Brainerd said it would take another twenty-one days to reach Dawson "more or less according to season, weather and condition of water in river and lakes, assuming that boats, etc., are available." It is good that he hedged on the time factor here because virtually everyone who was still in Seattle to read his words took months to complete the trip.

Before the gold rush, it cost an average of $150 to go from Seattle to Dawson City on the all-water route through St. Michael, and between $30 and $50 by ship to Skagway or Dyea. Brainerd estimated that the whole trip, outfit included, would cost no less than $500. Those prices increased dramatically and before long it cost up to $1,000 for a ticket to St. Michael and nearly as much to Skagway and Dyea. Scalpers routinely got that much for a ticket. Freight was $12.50 per ton to Skagway, $15 to Dyea and $200 to St. Michael with trans-shipment to Circle City, Fortymile or Dawson City. Freight bound only to St. Michael only was $100 per ton.

The combination of an opportunity to strike it rich and Brainerd's promotional campaign filled the trains to Seattle, and the streets were soon packed with people milling around trying to buy their supplies and get aboard a ship headed north. In some respects the whole thing was comical; indeed, when the naturalist John Muir saw the frenzied activity at Skagway and Dyea, he was so disgusted that he turned down a magazine assignment to describe the gold rush and told the editor the prospectors looked like a nest of ants stirred with a stick.

Dogs almost became an endangered species in Seattle because anything that walked on all fours was liable to find itself shanghaied into the harness of a dog team. Horses were bought by packers for use on the passes, and all sorts of inventions were proposed and shortcuts taken. Crackpots appeared as if from nowhere with schemes so outlandish that some people took them seriously on the grounds that anything that strange had to be true.

Frank Corey of Kalamazoo, Michigan, announced he was building a fleet of three-man hot-air balloons and sold several tickets for flights between Kalamazoo and Dawson City. The Jacobs Transportation Company of Seattle gave financial backing to Don Carlos Stevens to the tune of $150,000 to take balloons by ship to Tisklo Bay, near Juneau, and haul passengers over the mountains and down the Yukon River. History does not indicate that either man launched a balloon.

A Seattle newspaper sent a reporter north with several carrier pigeons. He attached stories to their legs and released them but none survived the trip back to Seattle. The Klondike Combined Sledge and Boat Company offered something called a "sectional steel sledge-and-barge," and outfitted it with sails, oars and air chambers for buoyancy. It also had burglar-proof compartments for storing the gold. It was tested by potential buyers and found to be totally useless.

One of the most touching participants in the gold rush was "General" Jacob S. Coxey. A few years before the gold rush Coxey was so irked with the lack of action by Washington, D.C., on solving the economic depression that he began organizing "armies" to march on the nation's capitol. He began his march on the West Coast and had people with him until about Ohio, when he began losing his recruits. He had drifted out of the news after that but now he was back again with a patented vehicle. It folded, it was held together with rawhide, it was "sectional collapsing" and it was all attached to a bicycle. "The plan is to load it with a part of the miner's equipment and drag the vehicle on four wheels for 10 miles or so," he explained. "Then the rider will fold up the side wheels and ride it back as a bicycle, to bring the rest of the load." It looked as convoluted as its description; it didn't work, either.

A New York chemist prepared a space-age food supply of capsules and tablets that "could be carried in a pocketbook" and weighed ten pounds. It produced scrumptious plates of soup, a quart of beef stew and a loaf of bread. Each button of coffee made a cup and potato lozenges produced a helping each. It was a great idea but it would be half a century before dehydrated foods became a wilderness staple.

A company sold stock for its plan for a school to train Arctic gophers to claw holes in the permafrost and relieve miners of the chore. A man named Thomas Arnold sought capitalization for his Alaska Carrier Pigeon Mail Service, delivering mail between Juneau and the gold fields. Somebody else designed a felt-lined portable cabin. Dr. Armand Ravol, the bacteriologist for the City of St. Louis, said he had germs on hand that would kill mosquito larvae as they hatched. Another inventor tried to sell X-ray machines that could detect gold.

One of the most pathetic dreamers was C. L. "Barrel" Smith of Houston, Texas, who wanted to go the most direct route from his home, which was through Edmonton, Alberta. The prairie town had been promoting an overland route north along the old Hudson's Bay route pioneered by Robert Campbell and his contemporaries. So Smith built himself a vehicle that had axles running through barrels rather than wheels. The barrels were loaded with about 1,000 pounds of supplies, and on top of this Smith built a wagon of rough lumber and put the remainder of his outfit aboard. He bought a team of horses and struck out across the muskeg. Before he had gone even a third of a mile the whole contraption fell apart, scattering his belongings.

One prospector, John J. McKay, got a lot of newspaper space from his stories about the good life women were leading in Dawson City. "There's but only one woman in Dawson City who is not married and she has refused every single man in town," he told reporters quite untruthfully. "They have knelt before her with uplifted hands full of gold. She wears short skirts, carries an umbrella and wants to vote."

Thus, America's worst economic depression ended virtually overnight as people started moving about again after a four-year sleep. Money came back into circulation, railroad cars were filled to capacity, ships went back into service, manufacturing resumed and jobs became available. The depression ended overnight in Seattle and the ripple effect gradually spread across the continent. Nearly fifty years later America would see the same thing when the Japanese attacked Pearl Harbor on December 7, 1941, putting a swift end to that decade-old depression.

CHAPTER 7

A Mariner's Nightmare

Before the gold rush struck, four Pacific Coast Steamship Company steamers ran between Seattle and Southeast Alaska on a scheduled basis, the *Queen*, *City of Topeka*, *Al-Ki* and *Mexico*. Others in service were the *Willapa*, owned by Alaska Steamship Company; the *Islander*, owned by the Canadian Pacific Navigation Company and the *Portland*, owned by the North American Transportation and Trading Company.

Two days after the *Portland* arrived, it made a return voyage, and three days later the *Queen* departed, and so it went all through the summer and into the fall and winter. Vessels that had been consigned to the bone heap were resurrected, repaired and sent north. A notable example of this was perhaps the eldest of the sidewheelers, the *Eliza Anderson*, which was built in 1858 and abandoned on tideflats for several years. She was immediately towed to the Moran shipyard in Seattle for repairs and put back into service. It had been said of the *Eliza Anderson* that no ship on Puget Sound was slower or made more money. She went north as part of a strange flotilla. She was joined by the sternwheeler *M. K. Merwin*, which was being towed by the tug, *Richard Holyoke*, one of the first seagoing propeller tugs built on Puget Sound. Also in the parade was the sidewheeler *Politkovsky*, which had been owned by the Russian American Company and turned over to the United States when Alaska was purchased, now being towed in tandem with the *M. K. Merwin* behind the *Richard Holyoke*.

This group struck out north, loaded to the gunwales with people, animals and goods, and the adventures began shortly after departure. The *Eliza Anderson* rammed another ship in Comox, British Columbia, and the parade headed to sea as soon as possible to avoid being detained by authorities. During a severe storm off Kodiak Island the *Eliza Anderson* ran out of coal and had it not been for a stowaway, she probably would have gone aground. A man had stowed away for a free ride to Unalaska, and when it looked like the old boat was going to go down, he came out of hiding, took command of the helm and steered them safely into a cove. Then he disappeared again. Years later when the whole story was told, it was learned that the man's brother had seen the near-disaster and rowed out in a rowboat to take his brother off the boat. The ships found coal in the cove and made it to Unalaska, where all the passengers packed up and left, opting for passage aboard a sealer instead.

Another ship of dubious record was the steam collier *Willamette*, which was quickly converted to a passenger vessel by installing six hundred berths in the coal holds without doing a thorough cleaning job.

Amid this frenzied activity, the longshoremen along Puget Sound went out on strike and became one of the few labor groups of the 19th century to win; their wages increased from 40 cents to 50 cents per hour.

Ships from all over North America and a few others bearing prospectors from Europe and South America converged on Puget Sound to join the flotilla. Many were unsafe. More marine disasters occurred between Puget Sound and Alaska during 1897 and 1898 than in all the previous years of shipping. Ships hit rocks and sank, they ran aground, they took on water and slowly sank, they lost their power or steerage, they were abandoned, they bumped into each other.

Berths were oversold and fistfights broke out between passengers or between passengers and crew. Mutinies and near-mutinies were common and skippers often carried sidearms for protection. Sometimes troublemakers were dumped ashore at villages along the Inside Passage. Stowaways were common because there were so many passengers aboard that nobody could tell the paying customers from the others. One man told of buying a first-class cabin but was unable to see anything out his porthole because a horse was crowded into a tiny space on deck among cargo and its rear end was flattened against the porthole.

Many ships struck out for Lynn Canal or St. Michael towing older ships that had been consigned to boneyards. Their upper decks were stripped off and the holds filled with cargo. Anything that floated was fair game for the Klondike.

The *Bristol* left Victoria with six hundred horses crammed into stalls so tiny that they can only accurately be described as upright boxes. The boat was also towing a paddlewheeler, and after the *Bristol* almost swamped, the paddlewheeler was cut adrift and left to fend for itself. The *Bristol* with its load of horses, and men crammed in here and there, continued northward.

So many complaints were lodged with the U.S. Customs agents about ships that were "carrying too much whiskey and not enough food" that they were forced to begin inspecting cargo headed north. To nobody's surprise, the agents found booze in containers marked sugar, coffee, kerosene and other food products. The agent in Dyea complained that "nearly every vessel arriving here carries twice the passengers the law allows it to carry and many of them are condemned craft that have been fitted up for this trade." As proof, he gave the example of a forty-five-foot launch appropriately named *Rustler*, which arrived with 70 passengers. Until only a few days before the ship got underway, its captain earned a living as a milk-wagon driver.

One of the oddest shipbuilding stories of the gold rush was the dozen steamboats built by the Moran Shipyard in Seattle. The paddlewheelers were almost identical and were built during the winter of 1897–1898. The contract for at least one being built for Standard Oil Company called for it to be 175 feet long with a beam of 35 feet and depth of the hold was 6 feet. The paddlewheels were powered by seven hundred horsepower engines and each also ran an electric generator. They had staterooms for twenty-four passengers but could carry more than two hundred "standees." They cost $38,000 each, FOB, St. Michael, Alaska.

The specifications called for them to be built with a flat bottom and straight sides and "The entire frame work, planking, decking and siding of hull and deck houses, shall be of Puget Sound Yellow Fir." Each vessel had three boilers set in sheet steel casing and lined with brick.

The main deck house was 142 feet by 33 feet and 10 feet high. A cabin, 36 feet long and 25 feet wide by 7 feet high, was divided into a dining room with state rooms on each side, a pantry on the port side and rooms for the captain, purser and a store room. Each state room had berths and a wash basin shelf with a water bottle and tumbler (glass) rack.

The main deck contained two hundred standee berths fitted with canvas hammocks, "all to be made as light and strong as possible."

Their names were the *D. R. Campbell, F. K. Gustin, J. D. Light, Mary F. Graff, Philip B. Low* (later nicknamed the *Fill-up Below* because it spent so much time under water), *Pilgrim, Robert Kerr, Seattle No. 2, St. Michael No. 2, Tacoma, Oil City* and *Western Star*, which was wrecked on the way north.

Three steamboats landed at the head of Miles Canyon to transfer their loads to the tramway that led past the canyon and Whitehorse Rapids to the town of Whitehorse. Photo courtesy Yukon Archives.

The construction was much easier than the delivery. Robert Moran, owner of the shipyard, decided to accompany the fleet of boats north. On lakes and rivers, the boats were graceful as swans, but on the rough ocean they became ungainly and dangerous, for they had absolutely flat bottoms and were not designed for the enormous stress caused by heavy seas. Taking them to sea was a big risk that Moran and his customers had to take. Shipping them to the Yukon River piece by piece might be more practical, but the business had to be captured while it existed.

The twelve-boat fleet had itself an adventure. It left on June 1, 1898, and eleven boats arrived nearly two months later at St. Michael, on July 27. One went aground on the Alaska Peninsula and was a total loss. A story persists that part of its pilothouse was used to build a church in the Katmai area.

Moran had to contend with drunken officers and rebellious crewmen. He had to fire some men along the route and always had the threat of maritime disaster hanging over him. Once they reached the Alaska Peninsula, wood for their steam engines was harder and harder to find. Storms bounced them around like wood chips, threatening to

53

swamp or break the boats' flat bottoms, but the remaining eleven boats were in good shape when they at last reached St. Michael.

Other steamboats were disassembled and shipped to the Yukon in pieces, then reassembled. Several were packed over Chilkoot Pass and assembled on Lake Bennett. According to the most complete compilation of steamboat records by the Yukon historian W. D. McBride, twenty one paddlewheelers were built on Lake Bennett. In fact, the first boat to arrive in Dawson City during the mad dash from Lake Bennett was the *A. J. Goddard*, which was packed plank by plank, brass fitting by brass fitting, over Chilkoot Pass, and then assembled on Lake Bennett. It was the first steamboat to go through Miles Canyon and down Whitehorse Rapids. It arrived in Dawson City on June 21, 1898. Another thirty were built in Seattle and taken north under their power.

CHAPTER 8

Outfitting for the Stampede

Perhaps the best way to appreciate the Klondike stampede is to describe what a typical prospector would have experienced on the trip, from his arrival in Seattle by train until he reached the Klondike gold fields. If he didn't receive one of the guides published by the Seattle Chamber of Commerce and given away all over America, he might have found a copy of an equally accurate guide published by the Chicago *Record*.

The Chicago Record's Book for Gold Seekers described the Klondike gold fields and told where the biggest discoveries had been made. Of equal importance, it accurately described the procedure of getting the gold. Although the discovery was made when nuggets were found on the surface, miners knew from previous experience that they would have to go down through layer after layer of geological history to get the remainder of gold beneath the surface.

The guide gave information on the various routes to the Klondike from Seattle obtained by a *Record* reporter named Omer Maris who had been sent to the Klondike in 1896. He described the three principal routes: The all-water route from Seattle by way of St. Michael, the Inside Passage route from Seattle to Skagway or Dyea, and the so-called Back Door route. This was the worst by far and perhaps should not have been even mentioned as an alternative to keep the desperate from using it. It originated in from St. Paul, Minnesota, then went to Edmonton, Alberta, and from there down the Athabaska River into Great Slave Lake, across it to the Mackenzie River, down to the Peel River, up to the portage over the Rocky Mountains and then down the Stewart River to the Yukon. The all-water route was 4,722 miles long, the Inside Passage route was 1,500 miles and the Back Door route was estimated at 1,882 miles.

Other possible routes were discussed—up the Taku and Stikine Rivers to Telegraph Creek and overland to the Yukon headwaters, across glaciers, but these were like the Back Door route, strenuous and unnecessary, even though Victoria and Vancouver merchants promoted it in an effort to steer stampeders away from the American routes at the head of Lynn Canal. A few parties tried it but, it was an exercise in futility like all routes other than the three classics —Chilkoot and White Passes, and up the Yukon River.

No matter which route they took, stampeders had to take at least a year's supply of food, and this fact was constantly impressed upon them by newspapers, steamship companies and certainly outfitters, who blended salesmanship with humanitarianism. One of the most widely distributed lists was made up by the Northern Pacific Railroad, which brought most of the stampeders west to Seattle.

Bacon	150 pounds
Flour	400 pounds
Rolled oats	25 pounds
Beans	125 pounds
Tea	10 pounds
Coffee	10 pounds
Sugar	25 pounds
Dried potatoes	25 pounds
Dried onions	2 pounds
Salt	15 pounds
Pepper	1 pound
Dried fruits	75 pounds
Baking powder	8 pounds
Soda	2 pounds
Evaporated vinegar	1/2 pound
Compressed soup	2 ounces
Soap	9 cakes
Mustard	1 can
Matches (4 men)	1 tin

Other items on the list included:
  Stove for four men
  Gold pan for each
  Set of granite buckets
  A large bucket
  Eating utensils

Frying pan
Coffee and tea pot
Scythe stone
Two picks and one shovel
Whipsaw
Pack strap
Two axes for four men and one extra handle
Six 8-inch files and two taper files
Drawing knife
Brace and bits
Jack plane and hammer
200 feet of 3/8-inch rope
8 pounds of pitch
5 pounds of oakum
Nails
10x12 tent
Canvas
Two oil blankets
5 yards mosquito netting
3 suits heavy underwear
Heavy Mackinaw coat
2 pairs heavy Mackinaw trousers
Heavy rubber-lined coat
Dozen heavy wool socks
6 heavy wool mittens
2 heavy overshirts
2 pairs heavy snag-proof rubber boots
2 pairs shoes
2 pairs blankets
4 towels
2 pairs overalls
Suit of oil clothing

Added to this were some medicines, additional clothing, reading matter, guns and ammunition and personal items. A surprising number of stampeders took cameras with them.

Cost of filling the list was estimated at $140 by the newspaper, but Seattle outfitters disagreed and said the total would be more like $1,000. The natural law of supply and demand soon made this figure modest.

By the fall of 1897 so many supplies had arrived in Seattle that they had to be stacked on the sidewalks. Photo by Asahel Curtis.

An item of extreme importance not on the list was a boat, because the outfitters and chamber of commerce assumed everyone would built a raft or a boat when they reached the headwater lakes. But the *Record*'s Omer Maris recommended that people bring their own canvas folding boats capable of carrying loads of two tons. Since most men in that period had a rudimentary knowledge of how to build things, they usually opted for building a boat or raft on arrival at the headwater lakes. Also, the prospect of adding a boat to the mound of gear they were required to take would have been a bit overwhelming. One company did import a stack of knockdown boats, most of which still reside atop Chilkoot Pass and are described later.

The *Record* guide also listed the customs duty collected by the North West Mounted Police at the summits of Chilkoot and White Passes, which was quite steep in some cases. For example, the duty on crowbars, knives, clothing and certain tools was 35 percent of its value. Almost nothing was less than 20 percent.

Armed with the various lists, the stampeders had to struggle through the hordes of people milling around downtown Seattle and the waterfront. Outfitters hired "steerers" to meet the trains and to circulate among the crowds steering customers to their stores. Two of the major outfitters were Cooper and Levy, and Schwabacher. The most successful retail chain in Seattle's history, Nordstrom's, was founded on the Chilkoot and White Pass trails by a Norwegian immigrant who earned his way north by repairing boots as he went along.

Once the stampeder had purchased his outfit, he would usually form a partnership with two or three other men because it was virtually impossible for a single man to travel alone with all that equipment. One needed partners to take turns standing guard at one cache of equipment while others packed it load by load up the trail.

The next step was finding a berth on one of the ships heading north from Seattle. Since this was decades before the government regulated fares, the cost fluctuated from hour to hour and was whatever the marketplace would bear. Men bought tickets to scalp them, and ship owners routinely sold more tickets than there was space. Fights broke out between men who had paid high prices for cabins only to find that they were already occupied by someone with duplicate reservations. The smarter ones went aboard as soon as possible and locked themselves in cabins and didn't come out until the ship was under way, and even then most didn't dare leave the cabin unoccupied, so they took turns going out, leaving someone to guard their belongings and to keep squatters from claiming the cabins.

Once underway, the trip up the Inside Passage was usually safe because the route is between islands and the mainland and is thus protected from the heavy storms of the North Pacific. Although record numbers of ships didn't complete the voyage, few shipwrecks resulted in the loss of life. Despite the lack of immediate danger, life aboard this fleet of Lazarus-like vessels was for the adventurous only. The holds were invariably full and goods were stacked along the passageways and on the open decks. Horses were wedged between crates, and pens of miserable dogs were stacked on the decks. Entrepreneurs had coops of live chickens, milk goats, sacks of potatoes and cookstoves for restaurants they would build along the route, and dozens of photographers came aboard with their enormous cameras, tripods, glass plates, chemicals and paper. Dance hall owners came aboard with their pianos, stocks of liquor, musicians and dancing girls. It was as much a migration as the one across the United States a few decades earlier along the Oregon Trail.

After reaching the far northern end of Lynn Canal, the stampeders faced the only overland portion of the trip. It was less than forty miles from tidewater to the headwater lakes across the border in Canada, but it was incredibly tough going because of the terrain and the amount of goods they were required to take into Canada.

The ships called on both Skagway and Dyea, eight miles away. Captain William Moore had stuck to his dream of making Skagway and White Pass the dominant overland route. For the past several years he had been spending winters in Juneau and living in his Skagway cabin during the summers while building a dock for the ships. Actually, the first dock he built was blown away by the winter winds that roar down the valley each winter, but Moore believed in his dream and rebuilt.

It hadn't taken long for the criminal element to discover Skagway and it was personified by Jefferson Randolph "Soapy" Smith, a conman and bully who had worked his way west across the United States, then up and down the West Coast between California and Seattle. He occasionally took a ride on one of the coastal steamers to Alaska to cheat people at cards and to promise to sell them things that they would never receive or things they didn't need.

On one such trip Soapy showed his ability to make influential friends. He was aboard the *Utopia*, of which Captain John A. (Dynamite Johnny) O'Brien was skipper. During the voyage O'Brien became incapacitated when a tumor burst while the ship was in Cook Inlet. A man who described himself as a former doctor performed emergency surgery on the skipper with scissors and a knife. After the surgery O'Brien was taken ashore to a hut because the ship was rolling so much in the bad weather that they feared O'Brien would be hurt. While he was recovering, the ship ran out of coal because the crews hadn't loaded her properly in Seattle. A coal station was nearby but the purser didn't have the $300 it would take for a load. O'Brien told the mate to dig coal from an outcropping they had seen at water's edge. After two days of the cold, messy work, the crew refused to continue, and O'Brien was too ill to go on deck and face them down.

Then Soapy Smith made his appearance, without giving his name, and asked O'Brien how he could help. O'Brien told him the situation and Smith loaned him the $300.

The *Utopia* got under way again and headed out into the Gulf of Alaska bound for Juneau. About eight hours later O'Brien awakened to silence; the engines were dead. The mate told him the coal they bought was no good and the engineers refused to burn any more. O'Brien had Smith sent to his cabin and asked if he could borrow Smith's pistols.

Soapy turned them over to O'Brien and the weakened skipper struggled on deck and told the crew there would be shooting if they didn't get the ship under way again. They stoked the boiler and soon were under way to Juneau, where they bought a supply of good coal.

This cemented the friendship between the men, and whenever Soapy or his men had to go somewhere, they always tried to sail with O'Brien. There is no record that O'Brien ever suffered from the friendship.

When the ships began disgorging people on Skagway's beach, Soapy steamed north aboard the *Utopia* with his friend O'Brien, and was there with a crew of criminals that included the Rev. Charles Bowers, a phony minister who gained newcomers' trust and relayed the information to Soapy. There was Billy Saportas, who claimed to be a newspaper reporter and had the job of interviewing newcomers to see how much money they had. Old Man Tripp, the nickname of Van B. Triplett, pretended to be a stampeder back from the gold fields to gain people's trust. Slim Jim Foster hung around the dock to help carry people's loads into town and refer them to his partners in crime for packing duties, after which their goods were stolen. Other members of his cabinet included Yank Fewclothes, King of Terrors, Jay Bird Slim, Fatty Green and Kid Jimmy Fresh. The U.S. deputy marshal was on the payroll, too. Soapy ran crooked gambling halls, freight companies that never hauled a thing, and telegraph companies that had no telegraph equipment.

Smith was very intelligent and he knew as much about politics as anyone who has been elected to an office in Washington, D.C. He told Skagway merchants and Territory of Alaska officials what they wanted to hear. When authentic journalists came through Skagway, Soapy rolled out the carpet for them and it paid off in favorable profiles in newspapers and magazines across North America. He formed charitable organizations for widows and children of men who lost their lives in the area, and his opponents were careful not to mention that some of those deaths were Soapy's fault.

Smith met his end on July 8, 1898, in Skagway, when a vigilante committee was formed to deal with the problems Smith and his men had been creating. It all came to a head when a prospector named J. D. Stewart arrived in Skagway carrying about $2,800 in gold he had panned in the Klondike. Apparently he let some of Soapy's men talk him into leaving his valuables in the hotel safe. When he returned for it, nobody knew what he was talking about. Rather than complaining and going away as most of Soapy's victims had, Stewart raised hell and went from person to person complaining about it. He refused to shut up and leave, as many people suggested, and apparently the time was right for something to be done about Soapy. Generally speaking, he had avoided harming permanent residents of Skagway, concentrating instead on the thousands of transients going and coming.

As Stewart's complaints reached every ear in town, a vigilante group called the Committee of 101 called a meeting and somebody sent for the U.S. commissioner across Lynn Canal at Haines. The committee gave Soapy until 4:00 P.M. that day to return the gold to Stewart. Gradually, all through that long day of July 8, the town armed itself against Soapy. Seeing that the wind had changed, some of Soapy's men sneaked out of town. Soapy couldn't do that. He armed himself with a Winchester .30/.30 saddle gun, a Colt .45 and a derringer and headed to a wharf where the committee was meeting.

At the head of the wharf he met a group guarding it, and down the wharf a short distance stood a man named Frank Reid, who had been critical of Soapy and his men and a leader in the Committee of 101. Reid walked up to meet him and they exchanged insults, then Soapy raised the rifle and pointed it at Reid's head. Reid grabbed it and pushed it down, and at the same time took his revolver out of his pocket and pulled the trigger. The hammer fell on a bad cartridge and Soapy fired the rifle, hitting Reid in the groin. Both men fired again. Reid hit Soapy in the heart and Reid was hit in the leg. Reid shot again and hit Soapy in the knee, but it was all over.

A crowd gathered and Reid raised himself on one arm and bragged that he got Soapy first. The crowd cheered and the rest of Soapy's gang ran for cover. Reid was in great agony from his wounds and knew he was going to die. When he was carried past his cabin on the way to the doctor's office, he asked them to let him see it one more time, then he begged the men to rub his wounded leg because it was cramping. He lived in agony for twelve more days before mercifully dying on July 20. He was buried in the city cemetery with a large headstone and Soapy was buried nearby with a very small stone. Naturally Soapy's grave is the most heavily visited.

CHAPTER 9

The Trails
Become Highways

As Captain William Moore had prophesied, the trickle of prospectors steadily grew, and in 1895 he talked a group of seven prospectors from California into using White Pass rather than Chilkoot, helping them transport seven tons of gear. Moore rented a string of horses from Dyea, brought them to Skagway on a raft and cut a two-mile trail up the river. He also shipped a sawmill in from Juneau and hired a crew to complete a trail along the Skagway River.

Then came the deluge. The first group came ashore in the last week of July and the human flood struck in August. Moore thought he was ready but he wasn't prepared for what did happen: The stampeders totally ignored him and the boundaries on his 160 acres. The newcomers, with the endorsement of the Commissioner for the District of Alaska, hired the surveyor Frank Reid, who in a short time would die with Soapy Smith in a shootout, to plot a town with sixty-foot streets and fifty-by-one hundred-foot lots. During this exercise, Reid found that Captain Moore's cabin was in the way of a street. Moore was told to move, and he refused. A group was appointed to tear down his cabin and move him. He and his wife tried to fight them off with a crowbar, but the committee won and the Moores moved. Four years later the U.S. District Court ruled in Moore's favor and gave him 25 percent of the assessed valuation of the improvements built on his and his son's 160-acre homesteads.

In the early part of the stampede, the White Pass trail was used by those who had pack horses or could afford to hire packers with a string of horses. The trail lacked the steep summit climb of the Chilkoot route, but it more than compensated for that omission with torturous conditions. It began innocently enough with a toll wagon road that followed the Skagway River four miles to a place where a town of sorts was built

More than 3,000 horses were killed on the White Pass Trail during the fall and winter of 1897, and this particularly bad area was called Dead Horse Gulch. Photo by Asahel Curtis.

called Liarsville. It earned this name because it was as far as some stampeders got, then when they came back to Skagway they told tall tales about the rest of the route they hadn't seen.

From the end of the wagon road the trail led up and down hills, through bogs, back and forth across the river, along a sheer granite cliff called Devil's Hill, then over Porcupine Hill, which had boulders strewn everywhere. The summit was at the end of a long hill of boulders and deep mudholes. The remainder of the route to Lake Bennett was more of the same, boulders, poor footing in muskeg, shallow streams to ford and finally about a mile of soil so sandy that it was like hiking on a dry beach.

Thousands of horses were brought to Skagway to be used as pack animals on White Pass, and the trail soon took on a Dante-like atmosphere with animals falling and screaming in pain as they broke bones; those that survived were seldom fed well enough to survive more than a few weeks. Some were never fed by their owners, so they slowly starved unless they could grab leaves and moss while they stood waiting for the line to move ahead of them. In one ravine alone more than 3,000 dead horses were counted, and the area became known as Dead Horse Gulch.

One stampeder wrote of walking past a horse that had broken its leg at a place where the trail went between two enormous boulders. The horse had been stripped of its pack and killed with a blow to the head, and left where it lay. The stampede continued across the horse's body and by the end of the day the only thing left of the horse was its head on one side of the trail and its tail on the other. The rest of its body had been ground into the soil by the stampeders.

Jack London was one of the many who wrote about the abuse of horses on this trail.

> The horses died like mosquitoes in the first frost and from Skagway to Bennett they rotted in heaps. They died at the rocks, they were poisoned at the summit, and they starved at the lakes; they fell off the trail, what there was of it, and they went through it; in the river they drowned under their loads or were smashed to pieces against the boulders; they snapped their legs in the crevices and broke their backs falling backwards with their packs; in the sloughs they sank from fright or smothered in the slime; and they were disemboweled in the bogs where corduroy logs turned end up in the mud; men shot them, worked them to death and when they were gone, went back to the beach and bought more. Some did not bother to shoot them, stripping the saddles off and the shoes and leaving them where they fell. Their hearts turned to stone—those that did not break— and they became beasts, the men on the Dead Horse Trail.

The Mounties detested the men who treated animals this way and the order was given to kill all animals brought into Canada that were badly injured. To avoid this, many owners stopped just out of the Mounties' range of vision and carefully covered the pack sores with blankets before proceeding. Fortunately, it was hard to fool the Mounties.

The other choice was Chilkoot Pass, which was the most heavily used, in part to avoid the Soapy Smith gang, and partly because it was easier hiking in spite of the steep summit climb. Also, the Chilkat packers were more reliable than horses owned by unscrupulous men, even if they did keep raising their fees as the stampede continued.

Unlike Skagway, Dyea had no natural harbor, so before winter a pier was built out nearly a mile to deep water. The ships had to anchor well offshore and unload onto lighters that in most cases were not much more than rafts. Horses were simply pushed over the side to swim ashore. The muddy beach was long and sloping, and after the lighter was grounded the load had to be carried a quarter of a mile or more to keep it clear of high tide.

Those with enough money hired Chilkats to take their equipment seven miles up the Taiya River in canoes to the first rapids, where canoe navigation ended. Here a town named Canyon City grew, and for the rest of the trip the goods had to be carried by someone. Those who could not afford to use canoes had to pack their loads along a trail that soon left the river for higher ground along the cliff on the south side of the river. Almost none of the trail in Alaska was level or easy to walk on. It wound up and down and around boulders, across streams and back up a steep climb on rocks covered with moss and mud.

The Chilkoot Trail in Alaska was broken down into roughly four stages: the five miles from Dyea to Finnegan's Point; two more miles to Canyon City; six miles to the last stop below timberline, called Sheep Camp; then three miles to the summit and the international boundary where the Canadian customs and immigration officers camped with the detachment of North West Mounted Police.

The going was much easier from the summit to Lake Lindeman and Lake Bennett with only one modest hill to climb before reaching Lake Lindeman. Otherwise, the trail followed a broad, flat valley past a chain of lakes, then dropped suddenly to Lake Lindeman.

The four way stations between Dyea and the summit developed quickly when the snow began falling that winter of 1897–1898. Until winter came almost nobody noticed a pleasant place five miles along the route where most of the Chilkat packers had forded the river. The first horse packers cleared a road that ended there. When the gold rush came the stampeders needed a place to rest, a man named Finnegan and his sons put up a tent and called it a restaurant. This was quickly joined by a saloon, a blacksmith shop and up to two dozen tents. Finnegan built a ferry to take stampeders across the Taiya River and charged them 50 cents for its use. Soon he built a footbridge to replace the ferry, but few stampeders used his labor-saving devices because in the fall the river was shallow and they could wade across.

The next stop was Canyon City, created because the canyon narrows at the first rapids. The site is one of the rare flat places along the Taiya River, and the river spreads out and becomes shallow enough to wade across. The area apparently was used as a rest stop by the Chilkats for centuries before the white men came.

When the gold rush began, a toll road was one of the first enterprises, and late in the summer of 1897 a toll bridge was built. Soon another bridge went in, this one built by Chief Isaac of the Chilkats. It didn't last long; it was demolished by a flash flood in September 1897.

During that fall of 1897 two companies appeared with plans to build tramways from Canyon City over the summit. The Dyea-Klondike Transportation Company and the Chilkoot Railroad and Transport Company built powerhouses on the west side of the river a short distance apart. The DKT group planned a road from Dyea to Canyon City, and the CR&T firm announced its plan to build a railroad from Dyea to Canyon City and an aerial tramway from there over the summit to Crater Lake. The announcement said the system would be in place by January 1, 1898.

The CR&T hauled a fifty-ton steam boiler by wagon to Canyon City and built a powerhouse around it. With these two companies going ahead with their plans, the Canyon City townsite took on a permanent look and the town was formally organized, platted and most of its twenty-two lots recorded.

Before all the plans could be realized, both tramway companies had to cut back their enthusiastic plans. A principal in the DKT group, Thomas I. Nowell, had a setback in a mine he was operating in Berner's Bay between Dyea and Juneau, and had to drop the proposed road while going ahead with the tramway to the summit. CR&T also reduced its plan by dropping the railroad to Canyon City. However, the company did some modest roadbuilding from Dyea to Sheep Camp. CR&T was finally able to begin operations in May 1898, hauling goods over the summit in large buckets suspended from the cables.

Canyon City's heyday was between February and April 1898, when the stampeders congregated there with their belongings that had to be taken on up the trail bit by bit. At that time the town had eight hotels, seven restaurants, five taverns, two supply stores, two storage tents, two tramway company power plants, two blacksmith shops, two barbershops, a real estate office, a doctor, a freighting company and a hay and feed store.

The town died almost as fast as it was born. When summer came in 1898, the stampeders were gone, and those who came along later hardly paused. If they had any money, they hired one of the tramway companies to take their gear from Dyea to the end of the tramway just over the summit at Crater Lake. Many of the buildings were abandoned and quickly scavenged for their lumber.

The stampeders' next stop was two miles upriver at a flat spot that became known as Pleasant Camp. During the gold rush a restaurant and hotel were built there, and a modest tent town came into being. The tramway crews probably had a camp there while they strung the electrical power and telephone lines to the summit. A few of the insulators and pieces of the lines can still be seen in trees, and sprockets and pieces of the tramway cable are on the ground.

The last adequate place to camp before timberline was Sheep Camp, apparently misnamed for the number of mountain goats killed in the vicinity by early hunters. It is thirteen miles from Dyea and three steep miles from the summit climb. By the first months of 1898 it was a large tent city. Unlike its neighbors at lower elevations, Sheep Camp had no wooden structures until the summer of 1897, when lumber was brought in and a hotel built. An early traveler said it wasn't much of a hotel because they charged for the privilege of sleeping on the floor.

Other wooden and log buildings quickly followed, a supply store, two restaurants, a saloon and and one or two grocery stores. Some early stampeders complained that the town was too tame because it had no dance halls or prostitution. This shortage was soon remedied, then quickly followed by problems of theft, which led to one public whipping and at least one murder. The Mountie's tough Sam Steele hiked through the town in February of 1898 and muttered, "neither law nor order prevailed, and honest persons had no protection from the gangs of rascals who plied their nefarious trade. Might was right; murder, robbery and petty thefts were common occurrences."

The public whipping occurred on February 10, 1898, when a mule-skinner named Billy Onions whipped Edward Hansen after the miners' committee found Hansen and a friend, William Wellington, guilty of stealing a cache of food and gear. The miner's court first sentenced them to hang, but Wellington committed suicide with his revolver. This had a chilling effect on the proceedings. The committee reconsidered its verdict and ordered Hansen to receive fifty lashes. After Onions had struck Hansen fifteen times, the crowd had had enough and asked Onions to stop. Hansen was taken down the trail to Dyea and put on a boat headed for Seattle with instructions to never come to the area again.

While most stampeders walked to Sheep Camp, contemporary accounts, undoubtedly colored by the promotional frenzy of competition with Skagway and White Pass, indicated that a road had been built all the way up from Dyea, but no traces of it have survived while the road to Canyon City has. Sheep Camp was also where many pack trains abandoned their pack animals when they were through with them. Some simply walked away from the abused, starving animals while others shot them to put an end to their suffering. Many stampeders commented on the number of pitiful horses and dogs wandering around the camp or lying dead nearby.

By first snowfall in 1897, Sheep Camp was a large town with two distinct business areas, one beside the trail on the east side and the other clinging to the banks of the Taiya River. By mid–winter it had at least sixteen hotels, fourteen restaurants, thirteen dry-goods stores, five doctors, three saloons, three transportation companies, two dance halls, two laundries and at least half a dozen other businesses. There was also a Chilkat encampment on the edge of town where packers lived and were hired to haul gear over the summit.

The next landmark, just above timberline, was called Stone House because an enormous boulder shaped something like a house with an overhang was the only place above Sheep Camp that provided any shelter from the weather. Many early travelers stopped there, and it was described in most personal accounts of hiking the trail. One of the most dramatic descriptions involved a prospector named Tom Williams, who crossed Chilkoot in December 1886, carrying news of the gold discovery on the Fortymile River. His companion was a Native American boy named Bob. They ran out of food and the Chilkoot crossing was too much for Williams; his toes were frostbitten and he could go no further than Stone House. The boy stayed with him and fed him dry flour, the only food they had. Williams grew weaker and contracted pneumonia. Bob loaded him on a sled and dragged him on down to Dyea, where Williams was able to tell of the gold strike before he died.

Stone House was erased when a flash flood hit on September 18, 1897. A lake of melt water had formed in a depression in a glacier high on the mountain over Stone House and early that morning it suddenly broke free. The wall of water came down and swept the big boulder away, and killed at least three stampeders. The whole area was changed considerably and the Stone House boulder was washed about a quarter of a mile down the canyon. No one knows its exact original location.

Just outside Sheep Camp came Long Hill, which some stampeders hated more than any other stretch of the trail. The way is marked by boulders of all sizes that have tumbled down from the steep mountains on the south side of the canyon. Footing was and still is difficult and the route goes upward relentlessly, sometimes forcing one to wade across the Taiya River, which tumbles noisily over the rocks.

The last stop before the summit climb was The Scales at the foot of the steep incline, the famous Golden Stairs. The Scales probably came

When the weather was good, stampeders formed lines up to two miles long to wait their turn to climb the Golden Stairs over the Chilkoot summit. The cluster of tents and cabins at the foot ot the steep climb was called The Scales. Photo by E. A. Hegg.

from the belief that Chilkats and other professional packers would weigh their loads here and increase their fees. It is one of the most inhospitable places along the route because it is in an open area with no protection from the weather; sunny, calm days are unusual here. As one stampeder later wrote, The Scales is "one of the most wretched spots on the trail; there is no firewood nearer than four miles. The wind blows cold, and everybody and everything is saturated. The tents are held to the earth by rock on the guy-ropes."

Apparently the first entrepreneur was one Peter Peterson of Juneau, who installed a rope tramway from The Scales to the summit during the summer of 1894. The tramway consisted of 10 sleds attached to an endless rope that operated on a gravitational system; sleds at the top were loaded with snow and released to pull the loaded sleds uphill. However, this device was installed on the alternate route over the summit, the Peterson Trail, which runs to the east, or right, of The Scales. The degree of Peterson's success is up for debate but it is known that the Chilkats were not pleased with his contraption and protested that he had put an end to their lucrative concession.

Peterson left the area for a year, but with the steady increase in traffic over Chilkoot, he returned and built another tramway in the spring of 1896, this one over the classic Chilkoot route, straight up from The Scales. This contraption used boxes atop sled runners. When a box was emptied at the top, he loaded it with snow as a counterbalance. If more weight was needed, he or one of his employees would climb into the box at the summit and ride it down while the payload went up. He charged 50 cents per load.

Competition arrived in the spring of 1897 when an old-timer named Archie Burns built a horse-powered tramway called a whim that required two horses going around and around. Burns charged 1.5 cents per pound, and it is possible that the scales Burns used led to the naming of the site. Before the year was over Burns had installed a steam-powered drum, and a gasoline-powered tramway. Part of this machinery remains perched at the lip of what is known as the false summit at the top of the steepest climb.

The visual symbol of the Klondike Gold Rush is the quarter-mile climb up the scree and talus slope that gained about one thousand feet in elevation. During the winter the climb was made in deep snow; in the late summer the main slope is free of snow and ice and one must scramble over stones and boulders of all sizes. Although there are routes over the summit on both sides of the classic route, the majority took the route dead ahead of The Scales, the well-named Golden Stairs.

In February 1898 two men carved a series of three-foot wide steps up the steepest part of the summit climb. They thoughtfully also carved out benches about every twenty steps so the stampeders could step out of line to rest without holding up the procession. They also strung a rope along the right side of the steps for stability. The fee they charged for using the steps is not known, and the total number of steps they carved has been estimated at thirteen hundred to fifteen hundred.

After reaching the false summit, the stampeders had another one-fourth mile of climbing up a gradual grade to the actual summit, where the Mounties and customs agents were waiting. The aerial tramway cables with their loads of goods creaked and swayed overhead and stopped at the summit. One of the tramways ended about a mile below the summit on the eastern shore of Crater Lake, where a large wooden crib was built to hold stones gathered from the area as ballast for the tramway. Unless they tried to sneak past the customs shack during storms or late at night—a few were able to do this, but only a few—stampeders paid customs duty to either Canadian or U.S. agents. If they bought their outfits in Vancouver or Victoria, in order to avoid paying U.S. customs, their goods had to be sealed while being taken from the beach

After the worst of the stampede was over and spring thaw was coming, the snow was so firmly packed on the Golden Stairs that the trench the climbers made lasted beyond the normal melting period. Photo courtesy Yukon Archives.

at Skagway or Dyea to the summit. And they had to hire guards to accompany it to insure that the seals weren't broken. If they bought their goods in the United States, they had to pay customs at the Canadian border. Somehow, someone would be paid

Once they slipped and slid down the snow bank to Crater Lake, their lives became easier again and they had level going down the broad valley to Lake Lindeman. Since it was easier traveling, there were few stops along this route. The first campsite of any consequence was five miles down the trail, a reasonably level spot on a ledge just upstream from Long Lake. It was called Happy Camp and during the height of the stampede it had a few permanent tents where one could buy food or perhaps a woman. Once stampeders reached Happy Camp, the rest of the hike down to the headwater lakes was easy.

CHAPTER 10

Surviving the Trails

Those who couldn't afford to hire packers or to use the aerial tramways were forced to lug their equipment to the lakes in stages. While one man stayed behind with the mound of goods, the others carried loads ahead and established a cache about a day's hike up the trail. It worked best if there were at least three men, four would be even better because there would always be someone at each cache while the others were on the trail. One stampeder counted the number of trips he and his partners made back and forth on the Chilkoot Trail and found that they had hiked nearly one thousand miles moving their goods the thirty-two miles to Lake Bennett.

It was for this reason that almost nobody who left Seattle in the summer and fall of 1897 was able to make the entire trip to Dawson City before winter arrived: It just was not possible to get all that gear to Lake Bennett, build a boat or raft and get it into the river before winter came. In fact, it took some nearly all of the winter to complete the transfer between Dyea and the lakes. So they were there all winter, trudging back and forth during good weather and holed up in tents and crude shelters when the rain and snow came down, or when the wind was so strong that they couldn't stand.

Most caches naturally were around Canyon City, Sheep Camp, the Scales, the summit and at various places between the summit and the lakes. Those on the Alaska side were natural gathering places for the stampeders, each about a day's hike apart, and each place became a village. From August onward the trail was a strange combination of hiking trail, migratory pathway, construction sites and villages. The unusual quickly became commonplace and it is interesting to note that in contemporary accounts those who came for only a brief visit described the trail in vivid detail, while those who were there for the long haul quickly accepted the unusual events as normal and wrote of the difficulties they were having.

Since it was almost impossible for the stampeders to get over the pass and down the river to the Klondike before snow came and the river and lakes froze, they settled into a life of trudging back and forth on the trail with heavy loads, holing up at night in tents, usually wearing wet clothing to bed. The weather in the summit area is almost always damp, windy and cold. Whiteout conditions are common the year around— blowing snow and clouds in the winter, blowing rain and clouds in the summer. Visibility is often limited to no more than twenty feet and the wind can knock a man down. Consequently, the stampeders were often halted for days at a time, waiting for a clearing.

It was a terrible winter for nearly everyone stuck on that thirty-plus mile bottleneck between saltwater and freshwater. There were murders on both trails—more in Skagway and along the White Pass trail than on Chilkoot, but both were subject to violence. There was an outbreak of spinal meningitis that killed several dozen; one account said seventeen people died of it in a single night. They suffered from pneumonia, other respiratory ailments, food poisoning, injuries from falling and from accidents with guns, knives and axes.

An interesting footnote to the whole gold rush is that while there were numerous murders on the American side, there were none on the Canadian side, nor were there murders in Dawson City, where the Mounties required everyone to leave their firearms in the Mounties' office. This strict control, which gave Americans fits, was under the command of a man whose devotion to duty was matched by his name, Superintendent Samuel B. Steele. He had established a reputation dealing with Plains Indians, bootleggers and assorted thieves before being sent to the Yukon to assist the detachment of Mounties already there. He visited Skagway and hiked over White Pass, then Dyea and Chilkoot Pass, and didn't like what he saw, especially in the Skagway area. He quickly learned to detest Soapy Smith and stated flatly rather than as a boast that neither Soapy nor his men dared enter Canada. They didn't.

As if the stampeders hadn't faced enough hardship, on Sunday, April 3, 1898, which happened to be Palm Sunday, a series of small avalanches occurred, one burying a family near the summit. Not long after they were dug out by neighbors, several people who were knowledgeable about avalanches began a flight down the trail toward tidewater, hardly stopping as they warned others to turn around. Few heeded the warning because they were willing to take that risk in favor of spending a clear, warm day transporting their goods over the summit.

At about noon the big avalanche came a short distance below The Scales on Long Hill, and it killed some seventy people—an accurate count was never made because the Americans weren't as well organized as the Canadian Mounties. Smaller slides occurred from time to time over the next several days, burying some people and killing a few of them.

The goods slowly accumulated in the summit area where the Canadian customs inspectors and Mounties kept careful records of each group's belongings. All had to register with the Mounties, and there was little chance that stampeders could get past them. An occasional stampede veteran wrote later that he was able to sneak past the Mounties at the summit by taking a long and hard way around them, but it was so strenuous and dangerous that the effort wasn't worth it. Only one or two storms were so severe that the Canadian officials had to leave their post for more protection at lower elevations.

Once everything had been taken to the summit and cleared by customs, the stampeders began the last leg of the journey. As noted earlier, it was easier because the trail is mostly downhill to the lakes, and more open. While horses were of no use on the Alaska side, they could be used on the Canadian side, and in a more humane manner. Teamsters built shelters for them, and packed in hay to feed them. They pulled wagons from the base of the summit at Crater Lake about five miles down to the head of Long Lake. Some may have gone another two miles to Deep Lake and it is conceivable that the teamsters found a way to get their wagons all the way to Lake Lindeman. It is more likely that the wagons went only as far as Long Lake and pack strings were used beyond there.

By the end of winter both Lake Lindeman and Bennett were surrounded by campsites, tents, lean-tos, cabins and hillside dugouts, and the most common sounds were of axes and saws as men chopped down the tough, stunted spruce trees and sawed them into boards to make boats. Here some fragile friendships suffered because of the way work had to be divided. The two-man saw used to cut tree trunks into boards was called a whip saw. To use it, a scaffolding had to be built to hold the log and one man while the other man stood below. The one working below was constantly bombarded by sawdust in his face, down his shirtsleeves, under his collar and in his hair. These manpowered sawmills are sometimes called the "armstrong mills," and everybody hated them. As the days lengthened into twenty-four hours of light and the weather warmed, the activity increased. Rain is not so common on the Canadian side of the pass and the stampeders wore dry clothing for the first time in several months. Long before the snow was gone from the lake shores and before the lake ice began turning blue in spots, many of the boats were built and waiting to be tested.

All through that winter rumors swept the shores of the headwater lakes while the stampeders waited for ice to clear. Once in a great while someone came upriver and over the passes headed for home or sometimes just to get out of the country. When these solitary, exhausted creatures appeared, struggling along behind their dog team, the stampeders descended upon them and hung onto their every word. Most of their news was bad news. They told of the food shortages, the almost unbelievably high prices for everything, and they also told how many claims had been staked and how many miners had been working there for more than a year. This may have stopped some of the stampeders, but not many. Anyone who had come that far wasn't going to give up easily, especially after living on a diet of rumors that usually were untrue.

Everyone didn't gather at the two lakes at the end of the trail. A few kept going and set up camp at the lower lakes—Nares, Tagish or Marsh— to get away from the crowds and to perhaps have an edge on the others when the ice broke. Some sold their outfits once they were past the Canadian officials and, traveling light, pushed on downriver on snow-shoes or pulling sleds behind them. Many of them built rafts just before the river ice cleared, ricocheted down the river and sold the logs for a nice profit in Dawson City. This mode of transportation was used for decades after the gold rush by people going to lumber-starved Dawson City.

Among the vessels built that winter on Lake Bennett were several paddlewheel steamboats that had been brought over the pass piece by piece, either dismantled steamboats or in something of a kit form. Many of these steamboats would remain on the upper lakes their entire careers, and some were in service half a century, until spur roads off the Alaska Highway and airplanes rendered them obsolete.

As spring inched into summer and snow cleared from all but the highest peaks, the ice slowly receded from the lakes. The weather was warm and the days so long that it was never completely dark at night. Still the ice blocked their way. To pass the time the stampeders, most of whom were young men, formed ball teams according to nationality or geography. They held footraces and other athletic events, and had sing-alongs at night.

Ice in the headwater lakes doesn't disappear all at once. When it begins melting it moves around as a single unit, breaks up into small floes,

Stampeders wait among piles of supplies waiting to clear Canadian customs at the summit. Aerial tramway cables can be seen just overhead. Photo by E. A. Hegg.

then reassembles into a pack blocking the small, lazy rivers connecting Bennett with Tagish and Tagish with Marsh Lake. Eventually the ice breaks up and becomes tiny shards that tinkle against each other and do not form barriers.

It wasn't until the second week of June 1898, that the ice cleared enough for the flotilla of more than seven thousand boats and rafts to depart confidently from Lake Bennett. They were rowed, paddled or sailed due north down the thirty-mile lake, past Caribou Crossing into Nares Lake, and then past a narrow entrance into Tagish. The Mounties had a checkpoint on Tagish Lake, where each boat had to register, and another at Miles Canyon.

In all, they had to go through nearly one hundred miles of lake before reaching the river itself. Once on the river they had fifty miles to go before reaching Miles Canyon. There the Mounties had another checkpoint and no boats could go through the canyon without permission from the Mounties. A notice was posted at the head of the canyon that stated no women or children were permitted to go through the rapids, no boats could go through until the Mounties had determined that they were safe and no boat with people in them unless the Mounties were sure they were manned by competent men. Violators would be fined $100. Some men hired on as guides, with the blessing of the Mounties, but Jack London was not among them, contrary to a legend that persisted for a number of years. London himself never made the claim. He went through the canyon late in the fall of 1897 and continued north as fast as he could because he was interested only in gold. He got as far as Lake Laberge, where he had to winter over.

Most vessels were unloaded at the upper end of Miles Canyon and the cargo portaged some three miles past the canyon and the rapids to the site of Whitehorse. An enterprising man named Norman Maculay built a wooden-railed tramway around the rapids and made a fortune charging $25 a boatload.

This was the last portage but it wasn't the last obstacle, because nearly thirty miles downstream lay Lake Laberge, the last of the lakes. Laberge has always been a tricky lake to navigate because it lies in the path of a confusing weather system that changes from minute to minute. Clear, calm and sunny weather can change in minutes to a howling storm. Hard winds from the Arctic can be replaced in seconds by equally foul weather from the southwest off the St. Elias Range, or even from the coast to the south. Thus, Laberge was the most difficult of the lakes for many boats, not necessarily in terms of danger but in terms of irritation.

Much of the upper Yukon system tends to be measured in roughly thirty-mile portions. The White Pass and Chilkoot Trails were just over 30 miles, Lake Bennett is thirty miles long, it is about thirty miles from Whitehorse to Laberge, the lake itself is thirty miles long, and the river that begins again at the north end of Laberge is still called the Thirtymile River even though it is officially the Yukon; this stretch of river runs thirty miles from the end of Laberge to where it joins the Teslin River at a former Native American town named Hootalinqua. The Thirtymile was the worst stretch of river to navigate because it is so swift, so crooked and filled with riffles, rocks and small islands. Today's river travelers constantly remark on its beauty. None of the stampeders noticed that, because they were so busy fighting to keep their boats and rafts off the rocks.

With Laberge and the Thirtymile behind them, the remaining 370 miles to Dawson City was relatively easy going. The river moves swiftly all the way into Alaska, and has only two sets of rapids to navigate, Five Finger and Rink rapids, neither particularly dangerous nor lengthy; a few bumps is about all.

Since there was little for them to do but drift along and watch for riffles so they wouldn't ground on sandbars, the stampeders had plenty of time to dwell on their partners' shortcomings. All fall and winter they had relied on each other and most had managed to submerge their irritations in their mutual need. Now with time on their hands, most dangers diminished and several months of resentful familiarity caused many partnerships to break up between Lake Bennett and Dawson City. A story persists that one island in the river was the scene of so many partnership dissolutions that it became known as Break-Up Island. The story may be apocryphal, but it does not exaggerate the conditions that existed.

Toward the end of June the first of the seven thousand–craft armada began straggling into Dawson City. If any of them expected a welcoming committee or a parade in their honor, they were deeply disappointed.

Assuming that most of the more than 7,000 boats registered by the Mounties at Tagish Post made the whole trip to Dawson City that June, it is safe to assume that an average of three persons were in each boat (this takes into account the many rafts that carried four, five or more). This means that twenty-two thousand more people descended on Dawson City before July 4, 1898, and most were no more welcome than the refugees that have been appearing on European shores in the 1990s from Africa and Eastern Europe. The Mounties almost had more than they could handle, and the streets of Dawson City were clogged with mankind all through the endless days of mid-summer.

Some stampeders who had a little money in their pockets took a look around, walked back to the river and caught the first steamboat down to St. Michael and home. Others sold their gear for whatever they could get and headed back upriver from where they had come. Others pitched their tents and tried to make a go of it. Only a very few were able to find ground to stake claims, and only a tiny percentage of those actually found gold. There were exceptions, of course, but for the most part the trip was a poor financial investment.

Some went to work for men who had good claims and others stayed in Dawson City to work wherever they could. Several hundred remained in the Yukon the rest of their lives, working wherever they could in order to remain in that remote but magical place where the sun never set in June and July, and where the skies danced and sizzled with vivid colors on winter nights, and where the silence was so intense it could almost be felt.

Men and women who were uncomfortable in the increasingly urbanized America found peace on this northern edge of civilization, and many never went elsewhere again. Among the most remote jobs was that of woodcutters for the dozens of steamboats that ran up and down the Yukon from late June through September. These men signed contracts to provide a certain number of cords of firewood for the steamboats. They spent the winters totally alone, except for an occasional visit by the Mounties, who ran winter patrols to check on woodcutters, trappers and assorted loners living far out in the bush. The woodcutters had daily company during the steamboating season, but when the last paddlewheeler pulled away from his camp in the fall, he had about eight months of solitude ahead.

CHAPTER 11

Fears of a
Starvation Winter

When discussing the stampede, it must be remembered how remote the area was and how long it took to get there. As a reminder, gold was discovered in August 1896. Nobody outside the area knew about it until July 1897, and it would be June 1898 before the first people leaving from Seattle and Vancouver would arrive. Thus, the miners already in the region had a two-year head start on working the streams that feed the Klondike River. The Klondike was so remote then that events occurring there can be compared with the adage of a tree falling in a forest; if nobody is there to hear it, there's no sound.

Before autumn of 1897, nearly everyone north of Southeast Alaska knew of Carmack's discovery. Nearly everyone loaded up their belongings and headed there. Miners from Juneau and Sitka, and all along the Yukon drainage system who did not have good claims already abandoned them and rushed to file new ones. Traders ordered more provisions to meet demand, saloon owners ordered more liquor and girls and the Mounties ordered reinforcements.

In the meantime, more fortunes were being taken out of the ground. More gold was being discovered along unstaked creeks, and the improbable was becoming commonplace. Prospectors who knew nothing about the conditions in the Yukon were sometimes better off because they filed claims where the old-timers said gold couldn't possibly be found, and made great strikes. This happened to a man named Oliver Millett, who believed gold could be found high on the hillsides above the valleys because, he reasoned, streams were once at the higher elevations before they cut through the hills to form the valleys. Sure enough, he made a big discovery on a bench over the valley and the area was named Cheechako (a Yukon word meaning tenderfoot) Hill. This created such a flurry of claim staking that the local Church of England minister grumbled that "the only benches not staked are those in my log church."

With the hordes of people coming into the Klondike, officials and storekeepers became justifiably worried because there wasn't enough food on hand to support the large population that had descended upon them. Although most had some experience in the North and could forage for food, there were still simply too many people for the supply of staples the merchants had on hand. Word was sent out to suppliers to send in more food, tons more, from Seattle to put aboard the steamboats that would come up from St. Michael in the spring. Emergency supplies were called for at the end of the summer of 1897, but when the last paddlewheelers arrived they had tools, firearms and booze, and very little food.

The Mounties and traders urged people to leave Dawson City if they didn't have food or good claims, and there was a quick and disorderly exodus of several hundred. Some made a downriver run in steamboats or their own boats, hoping to get all the way to St. Michael because there was very little food at the three major settlements along the route— Fortymile, Circle City and Fort Yukon. Others headed upriver, some in a steamboat, hoping to get back over Chilkoot Pass and down to tidewater before the winter storms hit.

The remainder stayed in the Klondike in what was a strange winter. Many of the miners were extremely wealthy by this time, yet couldn't spend it because they were so isolated and had very little to buy with their gold. Thus, gold lost much of its real value and they treated their dust and nuggets casually. They paid dearly for things that they did not actually need; lumber for a casket cost $40 a foot and nails $8.50 a pound, and when someone came into town with a woman's ostrich feathers hat, he was able to sell it for $280.00.

Because the Mounties and merchants had been able to talk many into leaving Dawson City, the famine didn't affect as many of the miners as originally anticipated. Ironically, while the miners survived, hundreds of Native Americans did not because they had become almost completely reliant on food from the traders and no longer prepared for winters without store-bought items. Lessons such as this were not lost on Yukoners and Alaskans; well into the middle of the twentieth century local law required storekeepers to always have enough food on hand to feed the entire region and avoid starvation winters. It was only after the Alaska Highway was open and maintained as a year-around highway and the air transportation improved that these laws were eased.

One of the oddest adventures related to the starvation winter that didn't materialize was the Yukon Relief Expedition. This came about because several prominent Alaskans, especially the missionary Sheldon Jackson and Captain Patrick H. Ray, commander of an Army detachment then stationed at Fort Yukon, insisted that the whole population of the Yukon River system was going to starve to death that winter. It was Rev. Jackson who conceived the idea of shipping in reindeer from Scandinavia to Skagway, Dyea and Haines and driving them over the mountains and down the river to the camps.

At the same time cooler heads insisted the starvation winter wasn't going to happen at all, including George Brackett, who had many friends in Washington, D.C. He argued that meat on the hoof was already on its way to the Yukon: three hundred head of sheep were at Fort Selkirk, two hundred head of beef cattle had gone over White Pass that summer, and several hundred head of horses and cattle were at the headwater lakes waiting for summer. If the people in the Klondike were starving, some of the cattle could be butchered and taken downriver by dog sled.

Washington, D.C., hounded by newspaper stories and letters from frightened relatives, went ahead with the plan promoted by Rev. Jackson. They placed an order for 539 reindeer from Norway. Accompanied by forty-three Laplanders, ten Finns and fifteen Norwegian herders, the reindeer went across the Atlantic by ship and were loaded onto rail cars in New York and taken across to Seattle. There they were loaded onto ships again and taken to Dyea.

After they arrived in Dyea and were put in an enclosure, Secretary of War Russell A. Alger decided that the starvation winter wasn't going to happen and ordered the Klondike Relief Expedition abandoned. An auction was held to sell off the additional food and tools assembled for the expedition, and then the reindeer were taken across Lynn Canal to Haines Mission. The Army, fearing the wrath of Rev. Jackson, pressed ahead with the plan to deliver the reindeer to Dawson City. It took them nine months to drive the herd over the trail Jack Dalton had blazed from Haines to Fort Selkirk, and then on down the river. With all the odd-ball events of the past two years, the arrival of a reindeer herd on the streets of Dawson City probably seemed quite normal to old-timers.

CHAPTER 12

A Woman
on the Trail

M ost of those who joined the gold rush real-
ized they were participants in an epic adventure, so it was by far the most
carefully recorded and photographed event of the 1890s. Many of these
people gained some fame or notoriety during or after the Klondike
stampede. It wasn't strictly a man's event, either; many photographs
show women on the trail and operating businesses. Two indomitable
Victorian women tourists, Mrs. Roswell D. Hitchcock and Miss Edith
Van Buren, went to Dawson City on a lark, and Mrs. Hitchcock wrote
an engaging, often humorous account of their adventure.

One of the Yukon's most beloved women from the gold rush into
the early years of the twentieth century was Martha Munger Purdy Black,
a Chicago-born beauty who had been married to William Purdy of Lake
Geneva, Wisconsin, for eleven years when they sailed for the Klondike
in June 1898. Her adventure on the way to Dawson City is one of the
few well-documented stories of a woman on the trail. Her book graph-
ically displayed the effect such experiences can have on a marriage or a
friendship.

She and her husband traveled with a large party and they arrived at
Skagway late in June. After spending several days sitting on the ship while
it unloaded cattle, miners' supplies and rails for the White Pass railroad,
they steamed on over to Dyea where the Purdy's outfit was dumped on
the shore. She later wrote that when she heard the ship *Utopia* reverse its
engines and head back toward Seattle, she knew she had burned her
bridges.

While they waited in Dyea, a generous young man gave Mrs.
Purdy his shack to stay in and he moved in with a friend. The men in
the party slept in tents. Shortly after their arrival, Mrs. Purdy's husband

put a few things in a knapsack and left to hike over both trails to see which would be best, and she remained to cook for the rest of the group. On his return, her husband pronounced Chilkoot as the best route and they set out on July 12 with a group of packers who had taken on the task of hauling their burden over for $900. They had gone only a quarter of a mile when they crossed the Taiya River on Kinney's toll bridge at one dollar per person. The owner got angry at them for not buying his steering paddles for $5 each because he said they would need them on the far side of the path.

Three hours after leaving Dyea they were at Finnegan's Point, where they bought cups of strong tea from a widow and her son. They reached Canyon City that evening, but kept going to Sheep Camp. Above Canyon City they encountered scores of dead horses and a shanty that they were told had belonged to two brothers who had died of exposure the previous winter.

At Sheep Camp Mrs. Purdy was given the only private room in the Grand Pacific Hotel, which she compared to her parents' woodshed. The hotel charged one dollar for the bunks and a breakfast of cornmeal mush, bacon and eggs, condensed milk, prunes and an orange.

As they climbed Long Hill, Mrs. Purdy almost overheated in her high buckram collar, tight corset, long corduroy skirt and full bloomers that kept slipping down. But she kept the pace of the men and her composure until they were near the summit, when she slipped and fell a few feet into a crevice. The fall cut her leg and she climbed out, then sat down and cried. Several men offered to help her; all except her husband, who said: "For God's sake, Polly, buck up and be a man! Have some style and move on!"

That really made her angry, so she got up, finished the climb and went into the custom broker's office and asked for a fire. "Madam, wood is two bits a pound up here," she was told. "All right," her husband grumbled, "I'll be a sport. Give her a five-dollar fire."

Thus fortified, the party cleared customs and walked on down to Happy Camp near Long Lake, where they ate a two-dollar supper of bean soup, ham and eggs, prunes and bread and butter. The bread wasn't done in the middle, for which the proprietor apologized.

The last two miles to Lake Lindeman were the hardest for Mrs. Purdy because the trail leads through a scrub pine forest and she tripped over "roots of trees that curled over and around rocks and boulders like great devil fishes."

From there they went on by boat to Dawson City. Her husband didn't think much of the place and soon left. By now, however, Mrs. Purdy didn't think much of her husband, so she remained behind and filed for divorce. When it was final, she married George Black, a civil servant who became commissioner of the Yukon Territory. The two became one of the most popular couples in Western Canada and her memoirs are among the most charming written about this period.

CHAPTER 13

Travels with
a Photographer

The Klondike gold rush was a boon to the fledgling photographic industry; it seemed every party had at least one camera, often more. It was certainly one of the most photogenic events of the period because the route north looked almost like a nation in retreat. Some of the best photographers in North America appeared on the trails and the river with their heavy loads of equipment and took photos astonishing for their clarity and composition.

This is all the more remarkable when one considers that roll film did not exist, and that the photographers had to mix the chemicals to coat the glass plates, then make the exposure, then process the plates to make a negative, and then, at last, make a print of the negative. All of this was done in tents during the daytime, sometimes behind trees on moonlit nights. Their devotion to craft is hard to believe.

One such photographer was Asahel Curtis, who was twenty-two when the stampede began. Curtis was the youngest of a family of three boys and one girl. One of his older brothers was named Edward Sheriff Curtis, and by the time Edward was old enough to vote, he had his own studio in Seattle, across Puget Sound from the family home near Port Blakley. Soon Asahel went to work for him as an assistant. Both boys were strong willed and they never got along well. Asahel found Edward bossy, and Edward thought Asahel was stubborn and ungrateful.

When the gold rush came, Edward made a deal with the Seattle *Post-Intelligencer* to supply them with photos of the stampede, and Edward sent Asahel to the Klondike to take those photos. Edward would remain in Seattle to capitalize on the new business flooding the studio. Stampeders wanted photos of themselves with their Klondike goods to send home. Storekeepers wanted photos showing their goods piled head-high outside their stores.

Curtis boarded the steamship *Rosalie* in the autumn of 1897 with his cameras, glass–plate negatives, chemicals, paper and clothing and headed north. The skipper was the colorful Captain John A. (Dynamite Johnny) O'Brien, the popular skipper who had befriended Soapy Smith. The purser was Charles V. LaFarge. Both seamen knew Curtis and took good care of him on the trip. LaFarge put Curtis into an empty stateroom and told him to keep the door locked and not to come out until they were well under way because the stateroom had been sold several times. Curtis did as he was told, and each night he dined with the captain and purser.

When they reached Skagway, LaFarge put Curtis in the first boat to go ashore, without his camera gear, which would arrive later on one of the lighters used to transport goods between the ship and shore. Before that could occur, a storm blew in and O'Brien weighed anchor and steamed down Lynn Canal for the sheltered water at Pyramid Harbor. Curtis stood on the beach watching the ship depart, feeling very alone. Of course, O'Brien brought the *Rosalie* back when the storm cleared and the cameras landed safely.

Curtis later wrote that Skagway was filled with newspaper and magazine correspondents, and some who just said they were. Most hung around town waiting to interview people returning from White Pass. A few were returning from the Klondike that fall and winter, but most were people who were admitting defeat and going home.

On Curtis's arrival, one of the correspondents asked him if he was going to the passes and Curtis said he was going all the way to the Klondike. "Ha!" the newspaper man snorted. "You won't get as far as Liarsville."

Curtis had his revenge. "Two weeks later they [the skeptical correspondents] wanted to buy my undeveloped negatives."

Not only did Curtis hike over the passes with his gear, he became the unofficial postman by picking up mail for men he knew along the trail; he returned to Skagway once with nearly one hundred pounds of mail. He inspired part of this mail by taking photographs, printing them as postcards and selling them for $1.50 each, a reasonable price at a time when a plate of soup cost one dollar and a plate of canned tomatoes cost two dollars.

All winter long Curtis alternated between the two trails and he was impressed by the wild country and the drama of the gold rush. He kept a diary sporadically, and sandwiched between orders for photos, recipes and formulas for photo chemicals, he waxed poetic on the harsh, beautiful land. An example follows:

Tales of the Yukon

Prelude—The mistic [sic] beauty of the mountain lake with the calm unruffled surface 'neath mountain crags with tiny cascades leaping merrily down from glaciers and ice fields above. The narrow winding of lake, more river than lake … .

Watching the throngs constantly changing what better could his chance be than that of the thousands who are before him. Seemingly every degree of the social scale has its representatives. Every possible kind of garb is to be seen.

Those who are elbowing one another represent every degree of wealth, from the richest claim holder to the poor unfortunate whose condition will compel him to go out.

The look of abstraction and gloom on many a face is heart-rending. The probable cause is the same in many cases; a mortgaged home or a farm or business that has passed into other hands [so] that the Eldorado could be reached. Those fair hills far away between which ran streams whose beds were pebbles of gold have faded. Weeks and months of hard work coupled with in many cases poor food have left the system weakened … .

Curtis had no burning desire to go on down to Dawson City; he was enjoying the drama of the passes and earning a good living taking photos of the stampeders, selling prints and keeping the negatives. Some prints were used as postcards, and Curtis was also the postman, mailing them in Skagway and bringing mail to friends on the trails. No record remains of the agreement with the Seattle *Post-Intelligencer*, and few if any of the photos were published. Nor is it possible to determine how many glass plate negatives he sent back to Edward's studio. Apparently he didn't send many because they were still in Asahel's possession when he died.

In March 1898, when winter had several more weeks to go, Curtis met two friends from Seattle on Lake Tagish—Eugene C. Allen and Zach F. Hickman. Allen was a printing salesman for Metropolitan Press in Seattle and Hickman was a printer for the same firm. They had talked the owners into staking them to a newspaper in Dawson City and sent Hickman up the previous winter to look over the situation. Hickman returned with the news that "gold is like flour up there. We'll clean up a million."

Allen and Hickman spent the rest of the winter in Seattle preparing for the trip. They spent two weeks training two dog teams hitched to sleds. Allen always had misgivings about the dogs because Seattle's dog population had been drastically decimated by the gold rush; the best and biggest had already either bought or stolen, so most of Allen and Hickman's training period was spent stopping fights, untangling harnesses and shouting until they were hoarse.

In February 1898, the two partners boarded the *City of Seattle* with their newspaper equipment and dog teams. Like most, they headed for the passes rather than the St. Michael route. They were certain someone else would see the need for a newspaper and they wanted to be the first down the river with a press. They knew they could travel overland with dog teams and arrive long before the first boats would arrive from St. Michael. They took a small press for job printing, a portable flatbed press for the newspaper, enough type for normal job printing orders, nonpareil type for the newspaper and enough paper to last a year. This was in addition to the required year's supply of food and $600 in cash.

Two more men had decided to join them in the dash: George Allen, Eugene's brother, and Ed Brandt, a relative of Hickman. Outside Skagway, Allen met a Seattle friend named Joe Dizard, who decided to accompany Allen and help him build a cabin to have ready while the other men came as fast as possible with the newspaper equipment.

Allen and Dizard were on their way to Dawson City when they met Curtis on Windy Arm of Lake Tagish. They had no trouble enlisting Curtis to go along and share experience in the area. The three men with a three-dog team pulling a sled struck out for the Mounties' Tagish Post, where they ran into problems because they were traveling too light. Allen and Dizard were traveling with only about two hundred pounds of food and Allen had only about $15 in his pocket. Curtis was carrying his camera equipment, a change of clothes, a few dollars and very little food.

It was a touchy situation because the Yukon ice was beginning to break and there were stories of men falling through the rotten ice and drowning. Allen was in a hurry to stake his newspaper claim in Dawson City, and Dizard was in a hurry to stake a gold claim on Walsh Creek, where he had heard a new strike had been made. It didn't make that much difference to Curtis because he was along for the adventure and would return to the passes after Allen and Dizard were safely on their way.

There was only one way they could get past the Mountie post at Tagish and that was for someone to go back to the post on Lake Bennett and get passes the Mounties there could issue to permit people to go down the river with less than the required equipment. Curtis volunteered to go for them since he had more snow experience than the others. It was sixty miles each way, on soft snow that made walking difficult and lake ice that was turning blue. Yet Curtis made the one hundred twenty-mile trip in only four days.

The next few days terrified all three men, and Allen later wrote that they were the most dangerous of the trip and perhaps of his entire life. The Mounties advised them to sit still for the next several days while the ice thawed but they were in a hurry and went ahead. Allen later wrote:

> After the snow got soft and the ice rotten, it was almost suicide to move over the Klondike Trail. We were now facing that danger with the advance of April. But Joe was all pepped up over that reported gold strike on Walsh Creek—which did not interest me at all—and I was just as determined to get to Dawson.
>
> What I wanted to do was get past the death-defying White Horse Rapids in Fifty Mile River [the Yukon between Marsh Lake and Miles Canyon] while I could still get across on the ice. That would let me get down to the foot of Lake Laberge, at the start of the Thirty Mile River. There I would be in a position to shoot that river on a raft into the Lewes River and so on into the main Yukon and to Dawson, while the other stampeders were held up on the lakes behind, waiting for the ice to break up.
>
> Fifty Mile and Thirty Mile Rivers were swift streams. The ice would break up first in them, while the lakes behind were still frozen. There was no trail on the right below Whitehorse because of the precipitous cliffs, so that to get below them the stampeders either had to portage around the right hand side of Miles Canyon, then cut across on river ice below the canyon, and portage around Whitehorse on the left hand side, or else it was necessary to wait until the ice was out of the whole river and shoot both Miles Canyon and White Horse Rapids on a raft, scow or in a boat.
>
> You can see what it meant to me to get down there and across the river between Miles Canyon and Whitehorse before the river ice broke up, and already the reports were coming in that the ice was going out any day, and was already too dangerous to travel on.

On April 8, 1898, the three men got up at 3:00 A.M. and began the dangerous three-day journey. They traveled ten miles down the river below Marsh Lake, and Allen said that the ice was breaking "like rotten cloth, and every step we had to watch that we did not plunge to death through an air pocket or a rotten spot." Several times during that day they were caught on floating cakes of ice—three men, three dogs pulling a loaded sled, all twirling down the frigid river in a dangerous Keystone Kops routine. Each time the ice broke free beneath their feet, they were able to jump to more solid ice or to shore without getting too wet. "Lord," Allen wrote in his diary that night. "I hope the ice holds up and gives us a chance."

Nobody slept well that night. They broke camp early and headed down the moving, snapping ice toward Miles Canyon, where the water was so fast that ice seldom formed. On the way they were struck by a severe snowstorm that held them up for a few hours. The portage trail around Miles Canyon led over a steep hill and when Curtis and Allen went ahead of Dizard and the dogs to scout it, they found the ice covered with flowing water.

"The ice is still there," Allen wrote in his diary, "but there is nearly a foot of water over it now and it may go out any minute. Lord, but what next is going to happen to us?"

The day was clear and the sun bright, and on the way back to Dizard and the dogs, Allen was stricken with snowblindness.

> This minute I can see nothing in the light and my eyes are throbbing as though they were being torn from their sockets, and I can hardly see to write these lines. Yet tonight we must work all night packing our outfits on our backs up around Miles Canyon and across that rotten ice below. No one but a fool would dare death like that, but we are going to make it!

The next day, Sunday, April 10, Allen wrote that he worked with eyes that throbbed incessantly, staying with Curtis and Dizard all night and packing everything over the portage. When they prepared to cross the river, water was swirling over the ice a foot deep or more. Allen took a stick and walked out onto the ice, paying out a rope fastened to a shovel handle anchored in the solid shore ice. He still could hardly see and suffered a mild case of vertigo as the ice swayed and bucked beneath him. He reached the opposite shore safely and fastened the other end of the rope to a tree so they could use it as a safety line. Then, the two other men carried their loads across. By the time their gear and dogs were across, the water was knee-deep. Allen later wrote:

> Hardly had we made that final trip when the ice went out with a sickening, crushing roar, and now the river between Miles Canyon and White Horse Rapids flows unhampered behind us. That was

the nearest I ever came to death, and about as near as I ever want
to get until my time comes. We're across! That's the big thing.
Nothing can stop us from making it through!

On April 15, the trio arrived at Lake Laberge where they caught up
with a rival printing plant they had heard was ahead of them. It would be
delayed until the owners could build a raft large enough to carry it safely. Allen
and Dizard made arrangements to float down the river on a large passenger
raft that was almost complete. Curtis turned around and went back to the
passes, taking the dog team and sled back to meet Allen's partners.

After spending a year on the trails, Curtis decided he should go on
down to Dawson City before freezeup in 1898. He stayed until the high
lakes began freezing. A friend from Seattle named Wesley Young was
with a group of young men on the White Pass Trail, and Curtis said he
warned them against trying to cross on the ice. They ignored him and two
men went through the new ice and drowned. He later told of being so
destitute at one point that he was walking along the river trying to get
the courage to beg for food when he found a few coins on the bank,
enough to save him the indignity of begging. Years later he also told of
watching a boat go through the Whitehorse Rapids that appeared doomed
because it went crosswise to the current and the dark figure at the stern
did nothing to help. At the last moment a side current caught it and spun
it back around with the bow into the rapids. Curtis said he was impressed
with the occupant's boat-handling abilities and he watched as it raced past
him. The dark figure in the stern was a large black dog, apparently set
adrift by accident.

Curtis hiked on down to Lake Bennett and joined a group of men
who were building boats for the trip downriver. He only identified one
of them in his diary and in photo captions—Charles Ainsworth. They
went down the river and that fall filed a claim at 60 Above Sulfur, which
means theirs was the sixtieth claim upstream from the discovery claim on
Sulfur Creek.

They built a snug spruce log cabin and put real glass in the windows,
probably some of Curtis's plates for negatives. The cabin was the only
worthwhile thing the men built; the claim was worthless. It was near the
stream bed and every time they tried to sink a shaft, the creek waters
seeped up into the hole. Like all Klondike miners, they worked through
the winter when the streams supposedly would be frozen and wouldn't
flood their shaft. They would build a fire in the hole, keep it going for

several hours, put it out and dip out the water, mud and ore-bearing gravel, then build another fire.

Because the creek was so near, to be safe they built a dam to divert it away from their claim, but as Curtis's diary entries show, nothing worked right:

> December 25, 1898: A little colder. Kept working on dam to freeze it as much as possible. Got a lot of wood. We had 2 hours' sunshine today. The success of our winter's work hangs upon this one thing; whether the dam holds or not.

> January 1, 1899: Watched water rise slowly. The bench on west side of Sulfur must have discharged gold on the surface and perhaps there is still a deposit on the hillside. This may be small but rich. Two small streams flow down the bank, each seeming to carry gold and at the foot gold is found. This is not on bedrock but on muck which also carries a little gold.

> January 3: Clean out for morning and evening fires. Day clear and cold probably about 30 below. A little water drains into hole each day but probably only the ice in the ground. Put in evening fire but do not light it until 9 p.m. When Charley goes to light he finds water dripping from northwest corner and so did not dare light a fire.

> January 4: Get up very late. Day cold. Water still dripping in hole and also forcing on top of ice. We cut a trench from below trying to tap the stream and although we get water we still do not decrease the force above the dam. Boys from 63 came down for a game of cribbage.

> January 12: Fletcher, Fredericks and myself go down to 57 Above. Go down in shaft. They seem to have bottomed the hole on a hill of bedrock. They have drifted off on three sides down an incline. In one place behind a boulder they found some pay. Bedrock seems in waves. A very thick layer of gravel. Later I was at 63 and down in shaft. They have gone through considerable slide and yellow clay. They went eight feet through bedrock and later came back up and built a platform. A very thin layer of poorly washed gravel. Depth of hole, 19 feet four inches; to windlass floor, about 18 feet. I fire No. 2 as we plan to sink it to bedrock if possible, otherwise we have decided to abandon the claim.

Curtis's last diary entry is on Thursday, February 16, 1899, when he had given up on the claim and was back concentrating on photography. Eugene Allen had planned for Curtis to work as photographer and engraver on the newspaper Allen founded, the Klondike *Nugget*, but the newspaper was never very profitable for Allen, although it outlived its competitors. Allen eventually lost it through bad investments.

"If I had a few more friends such as I have I would succeed very well," Curtis wrote as his last diary entry.

He went back to Seattle later that year after being gone nearly two years. He returned home very much his own man after the experience of the Klondike. He and Edward had a serious quarrel over who owned the negatives of photos Asahel had taken on the trip. They never spoke to each other again. Edward became the foremost photographer of Native Americans in history, and was underwritten by J. P. Morgan. Asahel operated a studio in Seattle for nearly four decades, documenting the growth of the city and much of the Northwest. He was one of the three founders of the Mountaineers, and resigned a few years later after several heated debates with club members on growth versus conservation issues. When he died in 1941, his children sent a telegram to Edward. Edward never responded.

CHAPTER 14

The Adventures
of Swiftwater Bill

For two years the Klondike was the place to be in North America. The promoter Tex Ricard was there. Alexander Pantages, who became a theater mogul, got his start there. Jack London lived a few adventures about which he later wrote so magnificently, and Arizona Charlie Meadows built the Palace Grand Theater in Dawson City. Dozens of other famous people wandered in and out of the region during its two years of fame, and the Klondike riches also created some of the world's most interesting turn-of-the-century characters.

Few were more fascinating than the frenetic William "Swiftwater Bill" Gates, the diminutive holder of more good luck than almost anyone else in the gold-mining business. His record of mining hits and misses, and wild love affairs, is something of an icon of Klondike madness. On the surface Gates' romances seem funny, almost Chaplainesque because of his diminutive stature and his breakneck way of life. But Swiftwater Bill pursued teenaged girls, he was a bigamist and he had at least one incestuous relationship. Every chronicler of the gold rush sees Gates a little differently, and this writer has always seen Gates an unhappy man pursued by his own particular demons, a man who made people laugh but never laughed himself, a man who could not sit still and could not enjoy his good fortune.

Gates was working as a dishwasher in a roadhouse in Circle City when he heard of Robert Henderson's big strike upriver at the Klondike. As soon as he heard the news, he took off his apron, threw his few belongings into a flat-bottomed boat and frantically poled his way upriver. He was then about thirty-five years old. He stood five-foot-five, and according to his biographer Iola Beebe, who was also alternately his mother-in-law, lover, accuser and demonic if not demented pursuer, Gates had a "scraggly growth of black whiskers on his chin, and long, wavy mustaches of the same color, curling from his upper lip." She might have added here that he was also irresistible to many women of all ages. He had received his nickname for boasting of his prowess as a steamboat man back in the United States, but he never had to work on a paddle-wheeler again because everywhere he looked he found gold.

His first claim was 13 on Eldorado Creek and he dug only a few feet before he found lots of gold nuggets. Being the kind of man he was, he could hardly wait to get to Dawson City to tell everyone of his good fortune. He filled several coffee cans with nuggets, worth about $400,000, and went into town to create a mini-stampede. The bars in Dawson City emptied and all the patrons fled to Eldorado Creek, where all remaining claims were staked from the source of the creek to its mouth.

While this was going on, Gates set about becoming the owner of the Monte Carlo gambling hall. This accomplished, he decided it was time to fall in love. Two sisters, Gussie and Grace Lamore, went to Dawson City from Juneau. They hiked over Chilkoot Pass and floated downriver on a barge and found jobs in a dance hall. As soon as he saw them, Bill outfitted himself in the most expensive clothes in Dawson City and went calling. In the dance hall he saw Gussie on the floor cutting the rug with a large French-Canadian and felt he had to have her. Love was immediate and complete. He went back to his own gambling hall, filled his pockets with gold and returned to the dance hall.

He arranged to meet Gussie and immediately after the introductions he told her: "I will give you your weight in gold tomorrow morning if you will marry me—and I guess you'll weigh about $30,000."

She turned him down, suggesting that they be only friends. Gates wasn't a quitter. By the next morning all of Dawson knew of Bill's romance, because he had told everyone he saw, and they knew him well enough to know they were in for a show. Gates pursued her throughout the winter with no luck. He grew desperate. During the spring of 1898 before the ice had cleared and the steamboats could bring in fresh food nearly everything was in short supply. Gates had been catering to Gussie's every whim and was getting very little in return. When she said she liked something, Bill bought up the entire supply in Dawson City for her. So when a trader showed up in a rowboat with two crates of fresh eggs, Bill knew that Gussie would want them because they had been breakfasting together for several weeks. But now they weren't speaking for some reason.

The owner of a restaurant bought the eggs and Gates went to him with an offer he didn't want to refuse. Gates offered $3 an egg, or $2,280 for all of them. The restaurant owner couldn't turn that down so he accepted. Then Gates told him to keep the eggs there and not to tell anyone he had bought them.

The next morning Gates went to the restaurant and ordered a dozen of the eggs, poached, and served on strips of toast. When Gussie came in she didn't look at Bill but ordered fried eggs. The owner told her they were all out of eggs because they were all bought up the previous night. Gussie was angry for a moment, then walked over to Bill's table and helped herself to the eggs on his plate, then sat down with him.

Even though he knew better, Gates continued pursuing Gussie and finally she permitted him to give her the $30,000 he promised her if she would marry him. She took the gold aboard a steamship and went home to San Francisco, banked it and wouldn't let Bill come near her again.

To get even, Gates next pursued Gussie's younger sister, Grace, and she agreed to marry him. They had their wedding in San Francisco, and he built her a $15,000 house in Oakland. While it was being decorated, they moved into the Baldwin Hotel. There he had a daily routine that was the talk of the town. He went to the lobby wearing a Prince Albert coat and silk hat, and stood around in all his glory. He paid the bell boys to point him out to other guests as "Swiftwater Bill Gates, the king of the Klondike."

The marriage to Grace didn't last long and she soon moved back in with her family without ever having lived in the mansion Gates was building for her. This really irked him, and one night he was seen leaving the house with a bundle wrapped in a bed sheet. The bundle contained $7,000 worth of silver plate and cut glass which he did not want his wife to have.

Deciding it was time to go back to the Klondike, Gates first went to Ottawa and talked the government into giving him a concession on Quartz Creek, then he went to England and bought a hydraulic plant to ship to Dawson City. On his way back to Dawson City with his hydraulic plant he stopped in Seattle and took a suite in the Butler Hotel. There he met his biographer.

Mrs. Iola Beebe was a widow of independent means and was the mother of two comely daughters. She wanted to invest in a hotel in Dawson City, and in the fall of 1897 shipped furniture, linen and other hotel equipment to Dawson City. It didn't arrive in St. Michael until too late to make the upriver trip before freezeup, so it was stored aboard a steamboat there waiting for spring.

A friend in Seattle told Mrs. Beebe that he could arrange an introduction with Gates, whom he said knew everybody in Dawson City and could help her get started. She went to the Butler and found it one of the busiest places in Seattle. Many of its guests were the newly wealthy from Klondike gold: George Washington Carmack, the discoverer-by-fault; his wife, Kate; brother-in-law Skookum Jim; Joe Ladue, the trader and sawmill owner and several other members of the northern fraternity were registered guests.

Gates was waiting for Mrs. Beebe in his suite, all decked out in his "immaculate black broadcloth Prince Albert, low cut vest, patent leather shoes, simmering 'biled' shirt, with a four-karat diamond gleaming like an electric light from his bosom." Mrs. Beebe continued: "I had left Bera, who was fifteen years old, in my apartments in the Hinckley Block and had taken Blanche, my eldest daughter, with me."

This may have been the worst mistake of her life to that moment because Swiftwater Bill Gates was immediately smitten with nineteen-year-old Blanche. Mrs. Beebe said Bill came across the thick carpet "as noiseless as a Maltese cat" and put out a hand that she described as soft and womanish, and he "spoke in a low musical voice, the kind of voice that instantly wins the confidence of nine women out of ten." She might well have added that she was one of those nine because this began her obsession with the man, an emotional condition that would stay with her long after Gates was gone.

He quickly agreed to help Mrs. Beebe on her arrival in Dawson City, then asked if Blanche would play the piano for him and invited them to dinner. Mrs. Beebe declined because she was uneasy with him, having read the newspaper stories of his adventures with women.

Three days later while she and Bera were getting dressed to go out, a friend of Gates came to the door and asked Mrs. Beebe if she and her daughters could join them for dinner at the Butler. She accepted, and nothing was ever the same afterward for the Beebe family. Gates launched himself into a romance with Blanche. She returned the ardor, telling her mother she was visiting a sick friend in the hospital while she was actually meeting Gates. It didn't take Mrs. Beebe long to discover this, but she was a few minutes too late. She visited the sick friend, found that Blanche hadn't been there at all, raced home to confront her and found the house a shambles—"It looked like a Kansas rancher's house after a cyclone"—because both Blanche and Bera had packed and taken off with Swiftwater Bill, leaving only a note: "We have gone to Alaska with Swiftwater and Mr. Hathaway. Do not worry, mama, as when we get there we will look out for your hotel." Gates had scored big: He had nabbed both Beebe daughters.

Mrs. Beebe went in hot pursuit and dashed aboard the steamer *Humboldt*, demanding that the ship's crew help her search for the girls. After knocking on nearly every stateroom door on the ship, they found the girls and hauled them ashore. Then Mrs. Beebe went after the perpetrator and finally found him huddled beneath a lifeboat. How he talked his way out of the situation was not recorded, but Mrs. Beebe found him a month later in Skagway when she was on her way to Dawson City over the passes rather than by ship around by St. Michael.

The inevitable happened. Gates conned the woman again, and a few days later Mrs. Beebe returned to her hotel room to find a note from Bera saying that she had gone with Bill to Dawson. "He loves me and I love him." They were gone and the chase was on again.

She didn't tell how she got to Dawson City, only that when she arrived she found her daughter and Gates were already married. When the first shipment of watermelons came down the river, Bill bought the first one off the boat for $40 and gave it to Bera, "simply to make his home that much happier," the mother-in-law wrote.

Soon Gates was dipping into Mrs. Beebe's bank account and borrowing money rather than working the vast claim on Quartz Creek with the expensive hydraulic equipment he had bought in London. Bill had a nose for gold, and a passion for spending. His debts increased through the winter, and to complicate matters Bera became pregnant and Bill insisted that she bear the child out on the claim. He offered a local doctor $2,000 to accompany them out to the cabin on the claim. Mrs. Beebe bought a case each of oranges and apples at $3 each, a $500 barrel of beer for Bill and accompanied them. The baby was born on the claim in the spring with the new grandmother in attendance and Bill paid the doctor $3,000.

The pitiful little party soon returned to Dawson City in a small boat that almost swamped in the frigid river, and soon it became apparent that Gates was broke again, not just out of money but deeply in debt, including several thousand dollars he owed to Mrs. Beebe.

One night they left the baby with Mrs. Beebe and said they would see her the next morning. But the next day one of Gates's friends told Mrs. Beebe that he and Bera had gone back to the claim to do some work. Three days later a messenger brought her a note from Gates: "We have gone down the river in a small boat to Nome with Mr. Wilson. I will send you money immediately on arrival there, so that you can join us." It was signed "Swiftwater." Then she remembered that the night they left, Bera had asked her mother: "You love the baby, don't you Mama?"

The next blow wasn't long in coming. A man came to the door with a deed to the house she had been living in. Gates had signed it over to him, and now he was evicting Mrs. Beebe. She got help from the Mounties, and stayed in the house until she could get a ticket on a steamboat for Nome, but her daughter and son-in-law were gone.

Bera had gone to Washington, D.C., where she had given birth to a second child, but now Gates had abandoned her and the baby. He was pursuing a young woman named Kitty, who was also his niece, and he had also started writing love letters to Mrs. Beebe.

This went on and on, and every time Gates came back into Mrs. Beebe's life, she always gave him more money. Once he showed up at her house, dirty and broke, and while he slept she washed and mended his clothes and pawned some diamonds to give him money to develop a claim on the Tanana River near Fairbanks.

He took off for Alaska without telling anyone goodbye, and typically made a big strike on the Tanana. Mrs. Beebe, who seemed to enjoy the chase, immediately took off for Fairbanks and found Gates, who promised he would pay her everything he owed. In the meantime, he paid her living expenses. Then she discovered that he was sharing his tent with his sister, who was also the mother of Kitty, his other wife. All this time he was still married to Bera. Nearby, Swiftwater Bill's mother was working as a cook for another mining outfit because her son wouldn't support her. His tangled life was enough to give Mrs. Beebe a headache, but she stuck to him.

When winter came she followed him back to Seattle on a steamer, and watched as he struck up shipboard romances. He kept neglecting to pay her what he owned, and as soon as the ship docked in Seattle he disappeared, partly because the Seattle papers had big stories about a bigamy suit filed against him by his sister. He was eventually found and brought to trial, but he managed to talk his way out of a prison sentence.

He also managed to talk Mrs. Beebe out of some more money, and again she followed him north to Dawson City, supposedly to collect it, but one suspects the chase had become second nature to her and also that she had some romantic leanings. Eventually, Gates decided enough was enough. He completely deserted his family and headed for South America, never to return. There he found more gold and made and spent a considerable fortune. He died in Peru in 1935.

CHAPTER 15

To Build a Railroad

From the very beginning the surveyors examining the overland bottleneck of Klondike transportation had railroads in mind, beginning with Captain William Moore who told William Ogilvie that it was possible but very difficult and costly to build a railroad over White Pass. So in 1898 the Close Brothers of London appeared in the North. They bought the railroad franchise from tidewater to the Yukon River that three men from Victoria, British Columbia, had obtained earlier from the Canadian government without enough backing to see it through.

The Close Brothers next acquired a right of way across the American portion by incorporating the Pacific and Arctic Railway and Navigation Company in West Virginia. Then the new company successfully lobbied Congress to extend the Homestead laws into the District of Alaska (this was before the Territory of Alaska was established) and provide for the right of way for railroads. At the same time the company was granted a charter in Canada to build a railroad from White Pass to Fort Selkirk and filed an application to extend the route past Dawson City to the 141st meridian, which was the international boundary.

The company made Samuel H. Graves president. At that time he was still building a reservoir in Colorado, so he ordered his chief engineer, C. E. Hawkins and John Hislop, Hawkins' assistant, to prepare to build the railroad.

Hawkins' first real task was negotiating with George Brackett for the wagon road Brackett had just built. Brackett was a former railroad engineer and one-term mayor of Minneapolis. He seemed to know everyone of importance across the country, and was in Skagway visiting a son when he conceived the idea of a toll road over White Pass. He joined forces with several other men, and Brackett was made superintendent of the undertaking. They intended to build a good wagon road to Lake Bennett with steel bridges across the Skagway River, using investors' money, of course. The undertaking was a disaster from the beginning. There were fights among the investors, between the officers, with competitors, between packers and the construction crews and between the federal marshal and Brackett. Almost nothing went right, although Brackett did manage to build a road of sorts all the way to the summit before at last running out of money.

When the Close Brothers began negotiations with Brackett to buy the rights to his toll road, Brackett thought he could hold out for a railroad of his own, but a good friend, Sir William Van Horne, who worked for the Canadian Pacific Railroad, convinced Brackett he should sell. He settled for an initial payment of $50,000 to cover damages or losses caused by the railroad construction, to be followed by another $50,000 for an option to buy the toll road.

Construction of what would become the White Pass and Yukon Route began on May 27, 1898, with Michael J. Heney in charge of construction. The project began with virtually no preplanning, and the officers of Close Brothers never once visited the place. The commissary department alone cost nearly $200,000 because there was nobody in the area to do the work and the company had to establish its own workforce. Nearly everything had to come from Seattle or Vancouver, including timber for the ties, bridges and trestles because the local wood was no good for the task. This imported timber cost $1 a foot. More than 450 tons of dynamite was used to build the right of way because almost every step of the way had to be blasted out of the granite cliffs. Most of the rails were supported on rocks because no soil existed along the route.

Heney's crews always numbered at least one thousand, and went as high as nineteen hundred. During the summer they worked in eleven-hour shifts around the clock for 30 cents an hour. Nearly all were on their way to the Klondike and needed the extra money, and many were well-educated or experienced men. Chroniclers tell of the company surgeon who needed some help while performing surgery and sent out a call for assistance among the men. A skilled physician was found working on the grade. He came back to assist in the surgery, then went back to work with his pick.

It was a tedious and dangerous process because almost the entire roadbed had to be blasted out of the mountainsides, and part of the agreement was that the Brackett toll road be kept clear so the Klondike stampede could continue. The gold fever caused the payroll to fluctuate wildly because the men would abandon the railroad the moment they heard of a strike, or even the rumor that there may have been a strike. In August of 1898 more than 560 men abandoned the railroad when they heard of the strike in Atlin. Within a week they began wandering back to the job because the Atlin strike was a small one, and like with all gold rushes, most newcomers were the too-latecomers.

Heney was the right man for the job because he was as tough as any man he hired, and he never hesitated to remind people he was in command. When Soapy Smith sent one of his men to pitch a tent for drinking and gambling, Heney ordered him off. The man said he had a right to be there. Heney didn't argue. He told his foreman that a rock protruding from the cliff wall above the tent "has got to be out of there by 5 tomorrow morning, not one minute later." The next morning the foreman, Hugh Foy, sent a gang to put dynamite under the tent and at 4:55 A.M. had a man wake Soapy's man, who only cursed and refused to get up.

"In one minute by this watch I will give the order to touch off the time fuse," Foy patiently explained. "It will burn for one minute and then that rock will arrive here or hereabouts." The sleepy man told Foy to go to hell. "I'm too busy to go this morning but you will unless you jump lively," Foy said, then shouted to the men above, "Fire!"

Foy hid behind a rock, and the tent owner quickly joined him; together they watched as the tent and all its contents were flattened by the rock shower.

Foy went to Heney's tent and told him the rock was down. Heney asked about the man and Foy said the last he saw of him he was walking down the trail in his underwear cursing. They weren't bothered again.

The track reached the summit on February 16, 1899, and the first train to the summit ran four days later. The line reached Lake Bennett on July 6, 1899, and the final spike on the railroad to Whitehorse was driven at Carcross on July 29, 1899.

This was the death knell for Dyea, the Chilkoot Trail and all the aerial tramways. Interest in the Klondike was waning and fewer and fewer stampeders were coming into the country by the summer of 1899. The Spanish–American War was under way and the newest gold rush was at Nome.

Accordingly, the railroad was able to buy out the four tramway companies for $150,000, and in the last week of January 1899, a crew went over to Dyea to begin dismantling the tramways, beginning at the Crater Lake end and working back to tidewater. It took until April to complete the demolition, as the crews used the cables to take out all they could. They had to leave most of the tramway towers and also left behind much of the cable and the boiler for the steam plant at Canyon City. By then it was all over for this Klondike visual signature and only an occasional curiosity seeker or hunter hiked along the trail.

CHAPTER 16

Those
Magnificent
Paddlewheelers

By 1898, steamboating was big business on the
Yukon, and the towering vessels had reached the state of the art well
before their arrival in the North. Skippers and builders had learned their
trades on the rivers of eastern Canada and the United States, then moved
west to the rivers of California, Oregon and Washington, as well as the
vast lakes of the Prairie Provinces and British Columbia.

They were so well engineered that it was said all they needed to float
was a heavy dew. In spite of the obvious exaggeration, the big boats built
for the Yukon were the result of the engineering demands of broad lakes
and fast rivers they sailed on before the Klondike stampede occurred. The
boats drew only a few inches of water. Because the water on the Columbia
and Snake rivers and the large lakes was deep and predictable, the most
popular boats were sidewheelers that dug deeper into the water; they
could even afford the luxury of keels. The Yukon boats were always
paddlewheelers because they required very little water to operate; the
wooden paddles protruded only six inches below the stern and they had
bottoms as flat as a frying pan. Consequently, the boats had to be trussed
up so their backs wouldn't break or become swaybacked. To accomplish
this, cables were strung from bow to stern and over a sawhorse arrangement
in the center, then periodically tightened or loosened, according to the
loads, to keep the bottom from buckling. They were something like a
whale in this regard—if they were beached their own weight could crush
themselves.

Each was equipped with a winch on the bow, which was used to
pull them through the swift Five Finger Rapids or to pull them off the
sandbars they inevitably struck. Accurate navigation was impossible on
the big river with its constantly shifting bars, and everybody took it in

The paddlewheeler S.S. Bailey *with crew and passengers, on the Fiftymile River. Photo courtesy Yukon Archives.*

stride when the boat ran aground. When this occurred a crewman would often wade ashore with the cable to hitch to a tree or a rock, and soon the combination of the winch and the paddlewheel pawing the water and gravel put the boat back into motion. Going aground was no particular crime for the skippers; everybody did it from time to time, especially late in the summer when the water level was low.

Nearly all the steamboat skippers who went to work on the Yukon had experience elsewhere, and often in more dangerous rivers. The main

Yukon had only the two sets of rapids to navigate—Five Finger and Rink—and those weren't much by riverboat standards. The major dangers or at least annoyances, were running aground on bars concealed beneath the murky water, losing control on the Thirtymile and hitting one of the many rocks or losing steerage control on one of the sharp turns and twirling like a dervish. The main Yukon didn't have the high speed and sharp rocks of the Columbia, Snake and Fraser rivers, but the worst stretch of river was the Thirtymile between Lake Laberge and Hootalinqua because here the river was both swift and crooked. More boats sank here than on the rest of the river combined.

The boats consumed an enormous amount of wood; one mathematician estimated that during the fifty years they operated on the river, they consumed more than three hundred thousand cords of the spruce timber growing along the river. Supplying the wood kept several men busy the year around, and woodcutter camps were scattered along the river all the way from Whitehorse to St. Michael. In some cases the woodcutters were failed Klondikers who either fell in love with the big silence of the Yukon or were unwilling to go home in defeat. Some never went home again, and poignant stories were told of those who did leave but got no further than Skagway before turning around and going back to camp. Sometimes an entire family would take on the woodcutting contract; the children would spend the winter in Whitehorse or Dawson City attending boarding school and living with a local family, then return to the camp when summer came.

A typical steamboat would have a crew of ten to twenty men: the master, a licensed pilot, chief engineer, second engineer, first officer, purser, steward, second mate, two firemen, two cooks, two waiters, two strikers or oilers, a night watchman and carry a deck crew of ten to twenty men.

Six-hour watches were normally held around the clock. The deck crew spent most of its time loading wood from the camps along the shore and then supplying wood from the stacks on deck to the firemen. A man was always placed on the roof, or hurricane deck, to extinguish any fires started by embers flying out of the furnace. Captain Edward Heckman, a former skipper once said:

> When you are consuming two cords of wood, mostly spruce, per hour there is a constant rain of live embers pouring out of the stacks. Stairways to the roof were covered by trapdoors. In heading for the pilot house ... it was advisable to lift the lid of the trap door and see

in what direction the sparks were flying before making a run for shelter. Many a good outer garment was ruined by live coals.

Captain Heckman once went to Dawson City in the winter to report to the steamboat *John J. Healy*, traveling from Whitehorse to Dawson City in a sleigh with twelve passengers, the mail and some luggage. The sleigh was pulled by six horses and they averaged sixty miles a day by changing horses at stations every twenty miles. His trip took five days. This sleigh route was first established by the White Pass and Yukon Route in 1902 and that year the trip cost $125 each way. Meals cost $1.50 and beds were $1 a night.

Known as the "Overland Trail," the route was hacked out of the wilderness by White Pass crews under a contract with the territorial government. The crews first cut down the trees, then used horse-drawn scrapers and plows to build a usable road. They had to build bridges and culverts, and cables were strung across the river occasionally for ferries. The company maintained up to fifteen posts along the route for overnight lodging, meals, fresh horses and repairs. Three years after the route was established, the 330-mile route had these stops (with mileages from Whitehorse shown): Takhini (22), Little River (40), Nordenskiold (62), Braeburn (84), Montagu (106), Carmacks (130), Yukon Crossing (152), Minto (175), Pelly Crossing (198), Humes (218), Stevens (236), Stewart Crossing (255), Wounded Moose (280), Indian River (303), and Dawson City (330).

On his arrival in Dawson City, Captain Heckman found three paddlewheelers wintering over in a slough upriver from Dawson City. It was a well-established site for the boats because the company had a cook shack, mess hall and bunk house for the crew. During the winter the black gangs (firemen and engineers) were busy overhauling the boilers, engines and pumps, and the deck crews had repairs and remodeling to do. Being an officer, Captain Heckman had nothing to do until the ice cleared.

The steamboat fraternity had found a way to keep the boats from being flooded when the thaw began and they were still frozen to the bottom. They partially filled the hull with water, then added steam to the water to make it almost boiling hot. This would free the hull from the ice, and deckhands could cut a trench around the hull so it could float. Thus, when the ice began breaking up in earnest, the steamboats would already be floating free in a small lagoon.

Captain Heckman told of a close call when one of the paddlewheelers, the *Hannah*, had not been stored properly the first winter that Captain Heckman arrived in Dawson City. She was supposed to be held away from shore in deep water by spars but the crew had neglected to take this precaution; when spring came she was frozen to the shore with about thirty feet of her bottom stuck to the river bottom. It was a race to get her thawed from the ground while the river began rising around her. Captain Heckman could only admire the carpenter who built her so strong and so flexible that she suffered no ill effects from being warped before finally breaking free.

The day before the breakup, Heckman and another pilot crossed the Yukon to Dawson City, and when they came back the ice was so rotten that they carried two long planks, shoving one ahead of the other so they would always be walking on one. There was also an "ice pool," according to Heckman:

> We, of course, invested in the ice pool at Dawson. A person could choose any minute of any day at one dollar a chance … . We, in camp, made up a small pool, twenty-four men each putting in one dollar and choosing one hour out of the twenty-four, regardless of what day the breakup occurred. The method of deciding the official time of the breakup was as follows: A post was fastened in the ice, near the center of the river. A long line with plenty of slack was fastened to the post and supported on stakes to prevent freezing. The line was carried from there to the whistle pull at the city power house. The blowing of the whistle decided the issue. Strange as it may seem, on this occasion [1907] the ice actually started to move in the morning but stopped short of sounding the signal. That same evening, between six and seven, she really let go and how I loved to hear that whistle blow, 'cause that was my hour, I'll have you know, and twenty-three bucks was welcome "dough" … It took sixty hours for the ice to pass Dawson.

Over the fifty-plus years the paddlewheelers ran on the Yukon, the crews became very adept at stretching the time the boats could be used. On the upper river, Lake Laberge was always a roadblock because ice would clear in the river both above and below the lake while it remained for additional weeks on the lake itself. The crews came up with a novel approach to overcome this problem; they dumped stove ashes, soot and used oil in a line down the lake and let the sun heat the dark material, which helped melt a track through the ice.

Another trick involved a considerable investment by the White Pass and Yukon Route on the river just below Marsh Lake. The company built a low dam with a lock on one side for small boats. The dam was used essentially for one thing: When the river began flowing in the spring but ice still clogged Lake Laberge, the floodgates would be opened on the dam and the force of the released water would flush away the ice, which had been weakened by the soot and ashes spread down the lake.

The steamboats nourished the major communities along the route to the Klondike. Carcross at the foot of Lake Bennett was already established because of the caribou that crossed there, as well as the good fishing in the shallow, short stream. But it would have been created by the gold rush anyway because its location was just right for the White Pass and Yukon Route railroad that came along after the gold rush, and a steamboat transportation system ran through the headwater lakes that led south to the gold mines along Tagish Arm and the diggings at Atlin.

Not long after the turn of the century the railroad with its fleet of steamboats had an efficient transportation system throughout the headwater lakes—Bennett, Windy Arm, Taku Arm, Grahame Inlet, Atlin, Tagish and Marsh—with Carcross as the major transfer point. The boats used on the lakes were small and were never used on the river.

The usual route for the steamboats was from Carcross down the full sixty-mile length of Taku Arm to its tip at the foot of the Coast Range. Here the steamboat tied up at a long wharf that was first built along the edge of a cliff but later straight out over the mudflats. The long walk on the wharf led to a special place called Ben-My-Chree, which means "girl of my heart" in Manx, which is the language of the Isle of Man.

The area was opened as a gold mine but the mine tunnel collapsed and the owners didn't reopen it. The next owners were Mr. and Mrs. Otto Partridge, immigrants from the Isle of Man. They once owned a sawmill on Lake Bennett, then they were partners in a steamboat company that ran small boats on the lakes. After buying the remote place, they began importing plants from all over the world and turned it into a garden. Eventually they made an arrangement with White Pass and Yukon Route to provide passengers with tea and cakes and rhubarb wine and to let them stroll through the grounds. After the Partridges died within a few months of each other, in 1930 and 1931, the White Pass and Yukon Route took it over and operated it until the last boat, the *Tutshi*, stopped running in 1955.

From Ben-My-Chree the steamboats returned north on Taku Arm to Grahame Inlet and followed the narrow lake to its eastern end where

The lake steamer Tutshi *at Taku Landing on Grahame Inlet. Here the freight and passengers loaded onto the small train pulled by the* Little Duchess *steam engine and were taken two miles to Lake Atlin. The* Tutshi *and* Little Duchess *were retired to Carcross, but the* Tutshi *was badly damged by fire. Photo courtesy Yukon Archives.*

the Atlin River enters. This place was named Taku, and a small building served as the depot for a very small steam engine, the Little Duchess, that pulled open freight and passenger cars along the Atlin River two miles to Lake Atlin. The modest railroad had no place to turn around so the engine pushed going one direction and pulled the cars the other. At Scotia Bay on Lake Atlin another steamboat, the *Tarahne*, loaded the freight and passengers and took them across the broad lake to the town of Atlin, one of the most beautiful settings in North America for a town.

It was a popular trip for tourists, and until the 1970s business cards were thumb-tacked two or three thick on the walls of the dining room at Ben-My-Chree. The two last steamboats on the lakes, the *Tarahne* at Atlin and the *Tutshi* at Carcross remained intact until the 1980s. The *Tutshi* was destroyed by fire in the later years of the decade. This lake transportation system continued until the mid-1950s when spurs off the Alaska Highway were built to Carcross and Atlin and air transportation became faster and more reliable.

The steamboats stopped running for good in 1955 when the *Keno* went downstream to be beached forever at Dawson City. At that time Whitehorse had the *Klondike, Casca* and *Whitehorse* on the river bank, but the latter two were burned by an arsonist in the 1970s, leaving only the *Klondike* intact in

Whitehorse. Along the river other bits and pieces of boats can be found: the bones of the *Casca* at Lower Laberge; the *Evelyn* on Shipyard Island just downstream from Hootalinqua; the tortured remains of the *Julia B., Seattle* and *Schwatka* downstream from Dawson City. On the bank at Dawson City is the small jewel of a paddlewheeler, the *Keno*.

Whitehorse was created because it was the head of navigation. Steamboats built at the Bennett boatyard that went downstream through Miles Canyon and over the Whitehorse Rapids never returned because none were powerful enough to fight their way up the rapids and back through Miles Canyon. So the town grew below the rapids where the steamboats from downriver could land, and this is where the railroad built its northern terminus. Since all passengers and freight were transferred between steamboats and the trains here, Whitehorse quickly became the most important town in the Yukon.

Towns appeared at the mouth of nearly every river that entered the Yukon, and those that were already in existence grew as traffic on the river increased. Moving downriver from Whitehorse, the first was Lower Laberge, where the lake emptied into the Thirtymile River. Unlike the rivers farther down the Yukon, the Thirtymile was named for its length rather than its distance from something.

At the end of the Thirtymile where the Teslin River enters is Hootalinqua, and immediately below it is Hootalinqua Island, where steamboats were moored and where one of them, the *Evelyn*, was abandoned and still stands. Next comes the Big Salmon River, then the Little Salmon, followed by Yukon Crossing, which was a roadhouse built along the route wagons used during the winter. Minto was mostly a native settlement and since it wasn't on a major stream, it wasn't used a great deal by the Klondike trade.

Next came Fort Selkirk, where the Pelly enters the Yukon. This was the Hudson's Bay Company post destroyed by the Chilkats and left abandoned for decades until the gold rush occurred. Its location was strategic because the Pelly was one of the alternate routes into the area, and some gold was found upriver. By the time of the gold rush, Fort Selkirk was a thriving village on the river, and it was the last major town on the river before Dawson City. Other villages grew at the mouth of creeks—Coffee Creek, Carlisle Creek, Kirkman Creek, Thistle Creek, Stewart Island—and most have survived in the form of ramshackle buildings, summer homes for Dawsonites, mining camps and even a few permanent homes.

The end came swiftly for the steamboats and Dawson City. The final blow was the Alaska Highway built during World War II as a supply route for the war effort. It officially began in Dawson Creek in British Columbia near the Alberta border and went through Whitehorse before turning west to Alaska. Construction of the highway was as dramatic as the construction forty years earlier of the White Pass and Yukon Route. It took only eight months to build the 1,523 miles from Dawson Creek to Fairbanks. Whitehorse grew rapidly during the construction and when it ended, the town was considerably larger than before, much larger than Dawson City, and more importantly, was on the major supply route. Now it had transportation by land, river, railroad and air, the latter a result of being chosen to be part of the Northwest Staging System, a line of airports that paralleled the Alaska Highway.

In 1951, with Dawson City's population at an all-time low of 783, the capitol of the Yukon Territory was moved to Whitehorse. Four years later the Klondike Highway opened between Whitehorse and Dawson City, and the last steamboat arrived in Dawson City in 1955.

Almost overnight the river was deserted. With no means of transportation other than their own boats, residents along the river had little choice but to leave. Two decades later, when I made my first trip down the Yukon, the furnished cabins stood empty of people, but still with curtains on the windows and dishes in the cupboard. Fort Selkirk had once been a town of about two hundred residents but in the mid-1970s only Danny Roberts lived there with his wife, dog team and small house dog. Occasionally, their daughter came home for a visit. Danny was on the government payroll to keep an eye on the buildings so travelers wouldn't strip them of everything or burn them. A few other people lived along the river, but probably no more than fifty along the whole five hundred miles from Whitehorse to Dawson City.

The only real town on the river is Carmacks, but it was built where the highway crossed the river. Otherwise, all the towns between Whitehorse and Dawson City are on the Klondike Highway, none dating earlier than 1955. Thus the river was abandoned as fast as were Circle City and Fortymile when the Klondike strike was made.

CHAPTER 17

Joe Ladue's Town

J oe Ladue could hardly have found a worse place for a townsite than the one he chose on the flat land just downstream from where the Klondike enters the Yukon. It wasn't a good place for a town because the land was marshy much of the year from water running down to the river from the hills above. During spring breakup the flat area was often flooded when the ice formed a dam and backed up the Yukon. It was several years before the town was protected by a dike along the river bank, and even then the town was still flooded from time to time. It was usually damp, which meant mosquitoes loved it. But it was reasonably level, which made it easier for Ladue to sell his lots, and it was easy to land boats in the eddy created by the Klondike running out into the Yukon.

At the beginning there were actually three separate towns on the Yukon River, with Ladue's town named for the brilliant George Dawson as the main one. Just up the Yukon River and across the mouth of the Klondike River was a settlement named Klondike City—known to most as Lousetown because the prostitutes were relegated to cabins over there. Directly across the Yukon River on higher ground was West Dawson. Another town named Grand Forks grew out on the gold-bearing creeks. It was founded by a formidable woman named Belinda Mulrooney, who took a look around Dawson City and didn't like the competition and living conditions. She headed out to the diggings and built a hotel and restaurant and quickly became respected and wealthy.

Dawson City didn't grow to a population of sixty thousand souls as much as it sprang, full-grown, like a character in Greek mythology, from the brow of the stampede. In June 1898, it had fewer than five thousand people. A month later it had a population variously estimated from sixteen thousand to a high of one hundred thousand; nobody knew

Lousetown, the uncomplimentary nickname for Klondike City, was across the Klondike River from Dawson City where it enters the Yukon. It was the low-rent district, and many prostitutes resided there. Photo by Asahel Curtis.

for certain, and even if a census had been taken it couldn't possibly have been accurate because so many people were coming and going that the downtown area more closely resembled a steamboat station than a town. At times Dawson City was called the largest city north of San Francisco and west of Winnipeg—but only for a few weeks.

It was also the most expensive city in North America. Eggs cost at least $1 each, milk was $30 a gallon, liquor was $50 a bottle and books cost at least $50. People paid for the pleasure of listening to someone read the latest newspaper, which might be months old.

Fire was always a major problem for Dawson City, and it suffered through three devastating fires and several smaller ones. The first occurred on Thanksgiving in 1897 when a dance-hall girl named Belle Mitchell left a candle burning in her room. It burned most of the downtown area and many cabins.

Another occurred on April, 26, 1899—caused, it was said, by the very same Belle Mitchell. This one occurred on a night so cold that men standing and watching it could hardly feel the flames that ignited their clothing. The Mounties took over the firefighting and blew up several buildings in front of the fire. This fire was by far the worst, but rebuilding began before the fire was entirely out, and when the breakup came, Dawson City again stood above the ashes.

Dawson City's flame of fame burned brightly for a year, then almost as suddenly as it was lit, several factors extinguished it. First and foremost, the thousands of stampeders who arrived in 1898 began leaving almost as fast as they came. Steamboats headed upriver to the dock at Whitehorse Rapids and downriver to St. Michael were filled to the gunwales with men and women fleeing the Klondike. Oddly, even though nearly all were broke and many in debt to supporters back home, they left the Klondike with a sense of accomplishment. At least, they seemed to feel, they had tried to improve their lives and had not spent the last year sitting back home wishing something would happen.

The Spanish–American War broke out in 1899 and the few young American men who stayed around quickly dashed home to join up. Some men who wanted to stay couldn't because they had no money, so they got back to saltwater any way they could; Chilkoot Pass and White Pass had a lot of two-way traffic from the fall and winter of 1898. The Nome gold rush also hit in 1899, and the same year British subjects had the Boer War in Africa as a source of new excitement.

During the first two years of its life, Dawson City quickly took on a veneer of civility, due in part to the strong presence of the North West Mounted Police under the leadership of Inspector Samuel B. Steele, who had led the hordes over the passes and down the river, and now was playing troop leader in Dawson City. Steele banned handguns, disorderly conduct, obscenity and card sharks. However, he permitted the dance halls, saloons, prostitutes and gambling halls to operate six days a week— Sundays were dead days in Dawson City. The Mounties were incorruptible, fair and unyielding. Misdemeanors were dealt with swiftly without benefit of due process because Steele was also the justice of peace. Minor crimes were dealt with by having the convicted man cut firewood for the Mounties' barracks and office: A favorite story involves the man who carefully chopped wood two inches too long for the Mounties' stove. Serious crimes brought banishment from the Klondike.

A strong influence was the quality of women who came into the area during the gold rush. The businesswoman Belinda Mulrooney founded Grand Forks out on the creeks. Martha Munger Purdy Black, a woman of great charm and humor, became the first First Lady of the Yukon Territory after traveling over the classic route with her insufferable first husband, then eventually marrying George Black, the future commissioner of the Yukon Territory.

Since the majority of stampeders were American, and the international

Front Street in Dawson City at about 9:15 A.M. in 1899. Photo by Asahel Curtis.

boundary was still in dispute, Canadians feared an American takeover of the Klondike. So the Canadian government sent a two hundred-man Yukon Field Force to Dawson City. They had nothing to do and eventually were disbanded so its members could enlist to fight in the Boer War of 1899–1902. However, the importance of the Klondike to Canada was obvious, and in August 1898 the Yukon Territory was established by the Canadian government with Dawson City the capital.

Still another factor was the quieting effect brought to town by the arrival of wives, children and other refined women. With the death of Soapy Smith in Skagway and the arrival of honest lawmen and judges, the entire route from tidewater to Dawson City was made safe for women and children by the end of 1898.

Two men who arrived in Dawson City with the other stampeders would soon make their presence known in histories of the Klondike. One was an Oxford don, Arthur Newton Christian Treadgold, a descendant of Sir Isaac Newton. The other was Joe Boyle, a fight promoter and sparring partner of Frank Slavin, the former Canadian heavyweight champion. Both men thought much bigger than single claims. They wanted enormous chunks of land that they would strip of its gold with the most modern equipment.

Already mining technology was changing. Various methods of thawing the permafrost were being tried, and the first method was steam. The first step was to clear an area of trees and brush, and then divide the area into grids. Workers drove pipes called "steam points" into the ground at specified intervals. Once in the ground, they were hooked to the steam supply and turned on. The system worked but it was dangerous to the workers (and equipment) because they could never be certain how much dirt was being thawed, and landslides and other accidents were common. It soon became apparent that the most efficient method was using cold water instead of steam, and high pressure hoses squirting cold water were used, much like fire hoses, to dig up the land.

Once the dirt was thawed, enormous dredges went to work on the loose rock and gravel. These metal behemoths were floated in artificial lakes made for the purpose, and they clawed their way through the thawed, exposed gravel, mechanically separating gold from the rocks and sand. They were as noisy as they were large, and could be heard for miles.

Shortly after the turn of the century everything changed. Treadgold and Boyle were able to get concessions to dredge large blocks of land and soon very few small operators were left working their claims with sluice boxes. Both men were able to get outside backing, and eventually the Guggenheim family took over and owned most of the mining claims in the Klondike. Working for wages became a way of life for most in Dawson City, and those who worked for the Guggenheim became known as the Guggies. The work wasn't nearly as back-breaking as before but most of the jobs associated with dredging could be accurately called hard labor. The dredges were enormous and noisy. They were too gigantic to be moved on land, so they moved by floating in special lagoons built for the purpose. They usually ran around the clock and caused an awful din from their engines, the steady gulping of rocks and sand, the clatter of the gold being separated inside and the refuse being deposited in the rear. As they worked their way back and forth across the valley floors, they left heaping rows of rocks and sand that made it look like a giant earthworm had attacked the valley.

During the first years of this century, many of Dawson City's residents went away to fight in World War I and didn't return, either killed in the terrible trenches of France and Belgium or unwilling to live on the edge of the wilderness again. The capitol remained in Dawson City but it was clear that the newer town of Whitehorse was becoming dominant.

In 1918, Dawson suffered its greatest tragedy. The big event of each fall was the departure of the last steamboat of the winter. Aboard it would be people leaving for the winter, students going back to school and a few people leaving the area for good. The departure of that last boat was always an emotional event because many were glad to see it go so that life could become quiet again. Others dreaded it because it meant seven or eight months of solitude and isolation. These feelings persisted even though by the 1920s it was possible to travel to and from Whitehorse because the White Pass and Yukon Route and other companies ran dog sleds and horse-drawn sleds, then "Cat Trains," sleds and wagons pulled by Caterpillar tractors.

In 1918, the last group out of Dawson City took steamboats upriver to Whitehorse, then the train to Skagway, where they boarded the *Princess Sophia* bound for Vancouver. The first night out the ship ran aground on Vanderbilt Reef between Juneau and Skagway, but the captain told would-be rescuers that they would simply sit it out and wait for high tide to free them. They sat there all night and nobody seemed particularly worried. The next morning at about 8:00 A.M. the ship slid off the reef, tearing a giant hole in the side. The ship immediately sank.

All 343 passengers and crew perished. More than 100 passengers were from Dawson City and most were employees of White Pass and Yukon Route and crewmen on the dredges. A gloom descended on Dawson City and it never really recovered from the loss. The town had become increasingly redundant as a center of government because the Whitehorse area was growing so fast that it made Dawson City seem more and more remote. It was only a matter of time before Whitehorse would become the capital and Dawson City's future would rely almost entirely on its past.

PART II

Today

CHAPTER 1

Rediscovering
the Klondike

After the steamboats were beached forever in the mid–1950s, most of the historic route to the Klondike lay silent and abandoned. Dyea and the Chilkoot Trail had already been ignored for half a century, and most of the river from the headwater lakes down to Dawson City ran undisturbed. Dawson City's population declined to around five hundred permanent residents while Whitehorse continued a steady growth.

Only a few recreational boaters and hunters and trappers used the river and it is doubtful that more than a hundred people hiked over Chilkoot Pass between 1900 and 1965. Occasionally a hunting party went up to the Canyon City area on horseback, only occasionally on up to Sheep Camp.

Not long after the demise of Chilkoot brought on by the White Pass and Yukon Route, a failed stampeder named Emil A. Klatt filed for a 160–acre homestead that included part of the abandoned Dyea. He built a comfortable home at the townsite and tore down the other Dyea buildings, selling them as lumber, windows and doors. He turned part of the rich bottomland into a farm, and as his produce business improved, he gave up on selling off Dyea's buildings and simply burned those that were in the way of his plows. He remained in the area until around 1920, then sold his property to Harriet Pullen, one of Skagway's most powerful citizens. Mrs. Pullen arrived in Skagway during the stampede with four little boys and $8, but by driving a team and wagon during the day and baking and selling pies at night, she accumulated enough cash to build Skagway's most popular hotel and become one of its most important citizens.

By the 1960s little remained of Dyea—the twin rows of piling stubs out to deep water, foundations of a few buildings, scatterings of rotten lumber, perhaps two or three cabins still standing and the Slide Cemetery where victims of the Good Friday Avalanche had been buried.

In the 1950s a logger got permission from the Forest Service to build a sawmill three miles above Dyea and log off some of the timber, but for the most part the forest lay untouched for decades, covered with snow in the winter, rained on during the summer and slowly covered with underbrush.

Although the White Pass and Yukon Route tracks didn't obliterate the entire White Pass trail, the presence of the trains discouraged most hikers from following the few portions of the trail still intact. More of the trail was obliterated by the Skagway–Carcross highway that put an end to Skagway's automotive isolation.

Chilkoot didn't come back into use until the 1960s the 1970s. The environmental movement and the international backpacking craze led to the rediscovery of foot paths and trails all over North America; it was inevitable that Chilkoot be among them. At the same time canoeing and kayaking came into vogue and people began launching them in the headwater lakes or in the river at Whitehorse. Some Yukoners made it a habit to go down to Dawson City by boat every summer, and during the fall, moose and caribou hunters used the river, all of which helped spread the word.

In the early 1930s, Alaskans began talking about the need for a park—with Skagway as the centerpiece—to commemorate the Klondike Gold Rush. Letters were exchanged between various Alaskans and Territorial Delegate Tony Diamond, who relayed them on to the National Park Service. The Territory of Alaska was treated with the customary benign neglect. Nothing happened until Alaska was admitted to the Union in 1959. Shortly after that happened, Charles Snell of the National Survey of Historic Sites and Buildings was sent out to Skagway and he fell in love with the ramshackle old town. Even though it was, and is, one of the few American pioneer towns made of wood that has never been destroyed by fire, Skagway was by then in poor condition: According to a local joke, the only thing that held up the precariously leaning Pack Train Inn was a city ordinance.

In addition to surveying and nominating several buildings for landmark status—including the old courthouse, the White Pass and Yukon Route depot, the Alaska Arctic Brotherhood building, Soapy Smith's parlor, the Pullen House, the Episcopal Church, the Presbyterian Church, Captain William Moore's cabin, Fire House No. 1 and the

Golden North Hotel—Snell suggested creating a national park in the area.

The buildings he listed were accepted by the advisory board and it, too, recommended national park status. The National Park Service began the slow process of creating the park that would eventually conclude in 1976, at which time the park consisted of four parts: all of downtown Skagway; everything from tidewater at Dyea to the international boundary at the summit of Chilkoot Pass; sections of the White Pass Trail that had not been demolished by the railroad and Klondike Highway construction and a unit in Seattle's Pioneer Square, in keeping with the role Seattle played in the gold rush, to be a combination museum, film theater and information center. The park wasn't an easy sale for local businessmen because they feared the loss of control over their buildings, and one reason many people had moved to Alaska was to get away from excessive governmental control.

During the development period the Canadian Parks Service, the Yukon territorial government and the British Columbia provincial government were working on a similar plan for the other half of the Chilkoot Trail. While the Yukon and British Columbia worked out details of land exchange—all of the Canadian Chilkoot Trail is in British Columbia—the Canadian Park Service worked with the provincial and territorial governments and the Americans on the Chilkoot Trail to continue the park from the summit down to Lake Bennett. The Yukon government crews built the trail along the lakes above timber line, and cleared a trail through the scrub timber from Deep Lake on down to Lake Lindeman, where they also built two log-cabin shelters.

Even though they received a lot of support for the international park concept, the Canadian Parks Service couldn't afford to declare a park covering the entire six hundred miles from Lake Bennett to Dawson City, so specific sites or relics along the way related to the Klondike story were preserved or restored. This includes the steamboat *Klondike* in Whitehorse; remnants of some villages, such as Fort Selkirk, along the river; the steamboat *Keno;* most of the gold-rush era buildings in downtown Dawson City and specific sites along the Klondike River.

This whole package, from Seattle's Pioneer Square to Dawson City, will be under the umbrella of the Klondike Gold Rush International Park, which is expected to be designated before August 16, 1997, the one hundredth anniversary of the discovery of gold in the region.

CHAPTER 2

The Inside Passage

Although few people traveling by boat from Puget Sound to Alaska think of the Inside Passage in connection with the gold rush, this is indeed part of the Klondike experience. The Klondike route from the major Pacific Northwest cities goes through some of the most spectacular scenery in the western part of North America. The Inside Passage is the accurate name given to this sheltered saltwater route that runs through the islands of Puget Sound and British Columbia's Gulf Islands between Vancouver Island and the mainland. Of the roughly one thousand mile route to the head of Lynn Canal, only about sixty miles is across open ocean; the rest of the route is on water sheltered from the North Pacific storms by clusters of islands.

This waterway is one of the world's most popular routes for cruise ships, and more than twenty ships from all the major lines as well as smaller, one-vessel lines sail the route during the summer months. Nearly all ships depart from the cruise-ship terminal on Coal Harbour in Vancouver, British Columbia. They cannot use Seattle as a base because of the Jones Act, which prevents foreign-registered vessels from sailing between American ports.

The Alaska Marine Highway system's ferries run this route the year around with extra vessels put on line for the summer season. British Columbia's ferry system has large vessels running on various routes from Victoria and Horseshoe Bay in West Vancouver as far north as Prince Rupert. All through the protected waters from Puget Sound north to the Gulf Islands, public and private ferries, small ships and passenger boats form a network of maritime traffic that makes it possible to visit many of the islands and remote villages.

The usual itinerary for the cruise ships is a late afternoon departure from Vancouver with the first night and following day devoted to

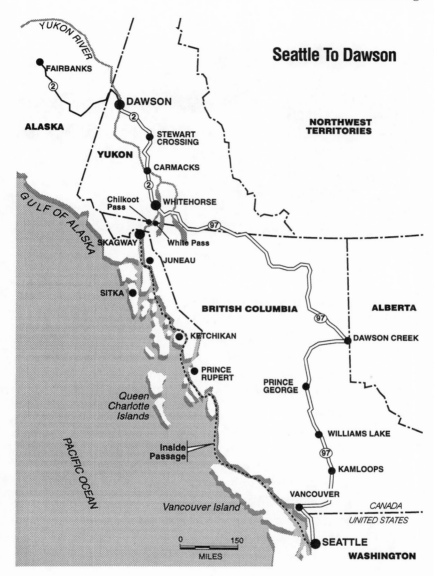

Seattle To Dawson

cruising through Canadian waters between the islands and past the tiny towns that look so large on maps. The first stop is usually Ketchikan, the southernmost town in Alaska. Here you can go for a walk along Creek Street, once the domain of prostitutes but now given over to shops and museums. Outside town are two parks with major collections of totems.

Other stops, depending on the itinerary, include Sitka, the former Russian capital; Petersburg, which has a large Scandinavian population; Wrangell, at the mouth of the Stikine River, and, of course, the capital

127

The tour boat M/V Fairweather, *which makes daily trips between Skagway and Juneau. Photo courtesy Holland America-Westours.*

city of Juneau. In this small city huddled beneath the mountains you will find excellent museums, shops and one of Alaska's most popular "drive-in" glaciers: Mendenhall Glacier is just outside town near the airport and on the way to Eagle Cove dock, where you can catch Holland America's *M/V Fairweather,* a two–deck passenger vessel that makes a daily round-trip between Juneau and Skagway. Mendenhall Glacier is much smaller than the monsters in Glacier Bay but the effect is the same. The *Fairweather* also passes several other glaciers en route to Skagway. Since not all cruise ships go into Skagway you may have to fly in on one of the small planes that operate between Juneau and Skagway.

The most popular way for backpackers and other budget travelers to get to Skagway is on the Alaska ferries. These ships leave Bellingham and arrive in Skagway four days later. Since cabin space is quite expensive and usually booked months in advance, the common practice is to pitch tents in various public areas.

CHAPTER 3

Skagway

O nce in Skagway backpackers go directly to the National Park Service headquarters at the foot of Broadway in the former White Pass and Yukon Route building for the latest information on trail conditions and trail maps. It is also possible to leave messages on the bulletin board for friends coming later.

Downtown Skagway has been restored to its turn-of-the-century appearance, and it is a very busy town during the summer months, with up to twenty cruise ships calling several times during the season, the Alaska ferries, the *M/V Fairweather*'s daily run to Juneau, steam and diesel trains coming in and out of the station next door to the National Park Service headquarters, fishing boats and the growing fleet of tour buses that take people in and out of town all through the day and into the evening. Guided tour groups cruise through town in regular buses, including the old-fashioned open-topped "gear jammers" that have been so popular in Glacier National Park for decades. You can also tour Skagway in horse-drawn carriages, in small vans or do it yourself on foot with a map. During the summer season, Skagway is as busy as it was in 1897 and 1898. Missing, however, are Soapy Smith and his motley crew. If you plan to stay in a hotel, you should make reservations before leaving home. Otherwise, you will be taking your chances and easily may have to pitch your tent in a campground.

If you don't go on a guided tour, you might want to take a warm-up hike two miles north of town to the Gold Rush Cemetery, where several people from the gold rush are buried, including Jefferson Randolph "Soapy" Smith and Frank Reid.

Another notable Skagway citizen buried with honors for a more friendly reason was Martin Itjen, who lived in Skagway from the gold

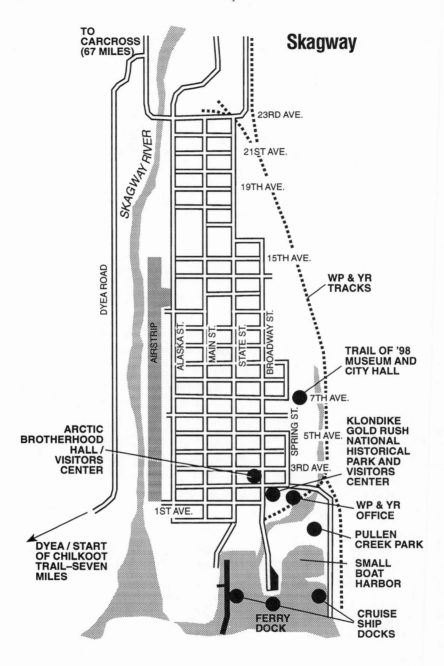

Skagway still bears most of its turn-of-the-century appearance because the majority of its original buildings are still standing. Photo by the author.

rush era until his death December 3, 1942. Itjen is called the founder of Skagway tourism, a title he richly deserved because he was tireless in his efforts to bring people into the Territory. Itjen built Skagway's first sightseeing bus and streetcars. His fleet of buses were attractions in themselves because he equipped one with a bear on the front that growled on command, and pointed left or right as the bus turned. Another had a manikin of Soapy Smith that saluted. Itjen also restored Soapy's Saloon and turned it into a museum, complete with a statue of Soapy bellied up to the bar. When the front door opened, the statue raised a schooner and red light bulbs lit up in its eyes.

As one would expect from a cemetery containing the remains of so many characters, this one has a boulder painted gold, which Itjen said was a gold nugget he panned out of the Skagway River, moved to the cemetery and chained to a tree so nobody would steal it.

The White Pass and Yukon Route shut down not long after the opening of the Skagway–Carcross Road, a spur of the Alaska Highway that goes over White Pass. As a freight carrier the railroad became obsolete almost overnight because trucks took over the job of hauling ore down to ships at Skagway's dock. To compound the matter, much of the Yukon mining declined and mines closed. On the other hand, tourism grew enough that in the late 1980s some of the passenger trains were taken out of storage, including a 1947 Baldwin steam engine that pulls the cars to the edge of town where a diesel takes over. The tracks were repaired, passenger cars cleaned up and service was restored between Skagway and Fraser, which is the international boundary station. Eventually rail service will undoubtedly be extended to Whitehorse.

CHAPTER 4

Dyea to
Sheep Camp

It is nine miles from Skagway to Dyea over a crooked and narrow road. A few backpackers hike over the road, but the heavy traffic on the dusty road doesn't make it an interesting hike; nearly everyone rides over in a taxi van. In 1991, it cost $15 one way. Once at trailhead, which is beside the steel bridge crossing the Taiya River, you have a choice of starting out on the trail immediately or strolling around the area to see the few remains of the Dyea townsite—a few collapsed buildings, the stubs of piling that ran a mile from high ground to deep water and the Slide Cemetery. If you arrive late in the day you may choose to camp the first night at the campground along the Taiya River and get an early start the next day.

The Slide Cemetery is where most victims of the 1898 Good Friday Avalanche were buried. A few others are buried there who did not perish during the avalanche. The graves and headstones are maintained by the National Park Service and the cemetery is surrounded by a wooden fence.

A register is at the trailhead. All hikers should sign it so the rangers will know who is on the trail. It is also a good way to know who your hiking companions will be and a good place to leave messages for friends coming later.

Although some people go over Chilkoot as though it were an urban footpath, the usual way to hike the trail is to take four or five days: day one to Canyon City (7 miles), day two to Sheep Camp (6 miles), day three over the summit and down to Happy Camp or Deep Lake (8 or 10 miles, respectively), day four to Lake Lindeman (3 miles from Deep Lake) and day five to Lake Bennett (7 miles). The strong and impatient hikers make the trip in three days: day one to Sheep Camp (13 miles), day two to Lake Lindeman (12 miles) and the remaining 7 miles out on day three.

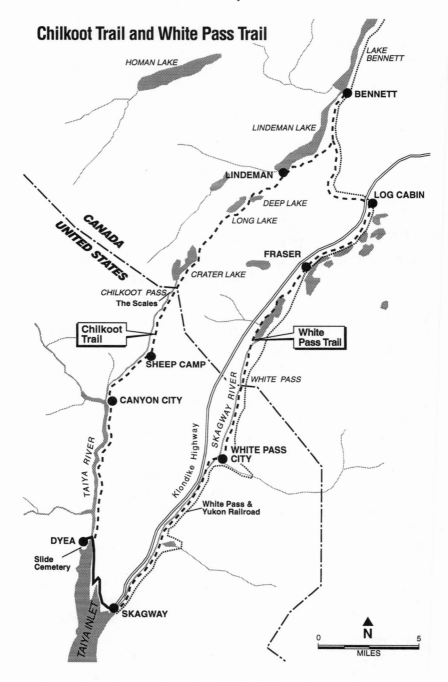

Chilkoot Trail and White Pass Trail

HOMAN LAKE

LAKE
BENNETT

BENNETT

LINDEMAN LAKE

LINDEMAN

DEEP LAKE

LOG CABIN

LONG LAKE

CANADA
UNITED STATES

CRATER LAKE

FRASER

CHILKOOT PASS
The Scales

Chilkoot
Trail

White
Pass Trail

SHEEP CAMP

WHITE PASS

CANYON CITY

SKAGWAY RIVER

Klondike Highway

**WHITE PASS
CITY**

White Pass &
Yukon Railroad

TAIYA RIVER

DYEA

Slide
Cemetery

SKAGWAY

TAIYA INLET

N

0   5
MILES

The American rangers and Canadian wardens have noted with deep misgivings an increase in marathon runners who make the entire trip in one day. Their speed isn't the problem. The way these marathoners charge down the trail like a bowling ball is.

When planning your hike, remember that camping is permitted only at these sites:

Dyea (Mile 0)
The sawmill site (Mile 3)
Finnegan's Point (Mile 4.9)
Canyon City (Mile 7.8)
Pleasant Camp (Mile 10.5)
Sheep Camp (Mile 13)
Happy Camp (Mile 20.5)
Deep Lake (Mile 23)
Lindeman City (Mile 26)
Dan Johnson Lake (Mile 28.5)
Bare Loon Lake (Mile 29)
Bennett (Mile 33)

The first 1.6 mile section is one of the toughest parts of the trail, mainly because you probably won't be limbered up. As soon as you leave the trailhead, the route takes you almost straight up the side of the cliff, much of the way over through heavy timber and over slippery rocks, around boulders and up and down steep pitches. Other parts of the trail are equally steep, but this rude introduction to Chilkoot shocks all hikers; some have been so intiminated that they turned around and went back to Skagway.

Almost as suddenly the trail becomes level again when it drops back down to the river level and joins an old road built to service the sawmill at Mile 3. A small shack, piles of sawdust and a few rough-sawn logs are all that remain of the sawmill. It is a good place to stop for a breather or lunch, but not a good place to camp because of the high population of mosquitoes and the fiendish no-seeums that thrive in the bogs and rotting sawdust.

The entire trail from Dyea to timberline just beyond Sheep Camp is through coastal rain forest with thick timber, heavy underbrush that includes enormous devil's club, moss-coated rocks and dozens of streams coming down off the snowfields and glaciers to the Taiya. Most of the river to Canyon City is relatively calm and free of rapids; those begin above Sheep Camp. Sometimes you will be so far above the river that you can hardly hear it and then you can listen to the wind in the Douglas fir or the streams coming down from the mountains; you can sometimes hear birds along the trail.

In these lower elevations you can expect to see butterflies, including the Monarch, which migrates to the Central California coast; hummingbirds; woodpeckers; the ever-present raven and Stellar jays. In the higher elevations you will see the camouflaged ptarmigan that would rather walk than fly.

After an easy stroll along the wagon road for three miles, the reality of the trail returns when the road ends at Finnegan's Point. No more easy going; from here the trail takes you along the face of cliffs, relentlessly up and down, through bogs and marshes, across streams and over moss-slickened rocks.

Then, at last, Canyon City appears on the far side of a bridge that spans a good-sized stream. Canyon City consists of a cabin with a stove and large porch where you can hang your sodden clothing to dry overnight (sleeping in the cabin is not permitted during the summer months). There is also a wooden rack for hanging food out of bears' reach, outhouses and several flat areas designated for tent camping.

About one-fourth mile upstream is the Canyon City townsite, reached by crossing the river on a sturdy footbridge. Most of the small artifacts have been stripped by hikers, leaving only a few larger items such as a cookstove and the massive boiler from the steam plant. When the park was first designated, the area was littered with bottles, cans, shoes, articles of clothing and decaying cabins.

The trail from Canyon City to Sheep Camp is unrelentingly rugged with almost no easy sections. It is up and down, along rock walls and through swamps, and in a few places you will have to half-climb and half-slide down steep pitches, clinging to tree roots for support. After a few hours of this, most hikers think longingly of the bare rocks they will have to scramble over above Sheep Camp.

Above Canyon City, you will occasionally see strands of telegraph wire along the ground or embedded in the trees, sprockets and cross pieces from the aerial tramways that ran from Canyon City to the summit.

The camping area at Sheep Camp is a virtual repeat of Canyon City, with an almost-identical cabin and tent-camping area. However, the cabin is in worse condition because it gets heavier use from people who hole up there for days at a time waiting for clear weather.

CHAPTER 5

Sheep Camp
to the Summit

The trail gets really serious after leaving Sheep Camp. Timberline is only a short distance from the cabin at the one thousand nine hundred-foot level. It isn't an immediate zone, like crossing a political boundary, but it isn't long before the evergreens disappear and only scrubby willows grow out of the rubble created by rockfalls from the sheer cliffs above. The Taiya diminishes to a broad stream that sometimes covers most of the canyon floor, forcing hikers to skip from boulder to boulder. At other times it is compressed into a rushing stream. The trail follows the right side of the stream until near The Scales, where it crosses on the snow bank that is almost always there.

This is the day of the most elevation gain. Sheep Camp is at about the one thousand-foot level and the summit is 3,739 feet above sea level; there's hardly a level spot in the 3.5 miles to the summit. Once above tree line, if the weather isn't foul, you can see for miles in all directions. However, I have hiked over Chilkoot four times and have had only one summit crossing without a drenching, wind-driven rain that fell sideways or clouds so dense the wands marking the trail disappeared. The pass is the slot through which the sodden marine weather from the Gulf of Alaska flows into the interior, and most of that moisture is dumped on the western slopes of the Coast Range before it can be taken over into Canada.

Snow covers the route above timberline most of the year and although rangers keep an eye out for unsafe snow bridges, it is a good idea to avoid crossing the Taiya River. Stay on the right side except when absolutely necessary. The rangers place wands with flags to mark the safest route; the wise hiker will use only that route. It isn't a bad idea to carry a pair of lightweight crampons for hiking in the snow, especially for downhill treks. A staff or alpenstock is at the very least a psychological aid.

Once you are above timberline on Long Hill, you can see frequent relics of the stampede along the left, or northwestern, side of the hill. Remnants of the tramways—towers, machinery and collapsed sheds—are along the cliff to the left. If you are hiking late in the summer more of the artifacts will be uncovered along the route, especially at The Scales. The Scales, the last stop before making the summit climb, is littered with artifacts—cables, sprockets, clothing, animal bones, and water-logged boards. Here stampeders threw away equipment and gear rather than pack it over the summit or pay the packers to do so. Most of these artifacts are hidden under the snow until August and September.

The dramatic part of the trail is directly above The Scales. Here, looming overhead, are the Golden Stairs, the visual symbol of the Klondike Gold Rush. This 45-degree climb is over scree and large boulders, an all-fours scramble up to the false summit. If you brought gloves, you will be glad you did so. During the summer, with the snow gone, the climb looks quite different from the historical photos. Now you will see only dark and rain-slickened boulders. It is also a tougher climb on the boulders than up the steps carved out by the stampeders.

The National Park Service has strips of orange plastic tied to the rocks and on wands to lead you upward. During the late summer when all the snow is gone, you can go over the boulders or along the side of the notch and use the steel cables to help pull you along, but this is rough on hands and gloves. Follow the route marked by rangers.

Once you reach the top of the Golden Stairs, you have reached the false summit and are still about a quarter of a mile from the real summit; but at least you can walk upright rather than crawling along on all fours. At the false summit you will see part of an engine, presumably from the first of the tramways that was a continuous cable with sleds attached. The false summit also has a great view of The Scales, Long Hill and the surrounding mountain ranges—in clear weather, of course. The remainder of the climb to the top is nothing more or less than a trudge up a steep grade.

Shortly before you reach the summit, you will note a long, flat ledge on the east, or right, side of the trail just before you reach the international boundary marker. Atop this ledge is one of the many mysteries of Chilkoot; more than eighty knockdown boats were left up there during the stampede.

They are made of canvas with wooden frames, and the connecting hardware is brass. We'll probably never be certain of their origin, but Frank Norris, the historian and writer in the National Park Service's

Anchorage office, has researched the matter as thoroughly as possible and arrived at the conclusion that they were shipped in by a firm named Flowers, Smith and Company.

This group, led by John M. Flowers and F. L. M. Smith, was an aggressive company that laid out a thirty-two-block town on Lake Lindeman. In their paperwork, they gave their address as Lake Lindeman, Alaska, because the international boundary wasn't yet established in 1897. Flowers built a dock and warehouse on the lake and awarded himself one of the blocks that had two hundred square feet on the lakeshore and a commanding view from a bluff.

Flowers and Smith owned a string of horses they marched over the pass to be used in pack trains from the summit to Lake Lindeman and perhaps Lake Bennett. They also announced they would operate a forty-six-foot launch to run the length of Lake Lindeman.

They aggressively promoted their knockdown boats, calling them "non pareil canvas compartment boats," suitable for one man. They were about 17.5 feet long and 5 feet wide. Their advertisements claimed that the boats were packed in "crates of convenient size and weight to transport across the passes without inconvenience."

Nobody knows exactly why they were left at the summit, although some suspect the boats weren't very useful because they were too small to carry a good load. Others believe the Mounties stopped them because they were so shoddily built that they would be dangerous on the lakes and river.

The most likely reason, according to Norris, is that the Mounties evicted Flowers and Smith from their property on Lake Lindeman in February 1898 because they were doing business as Americans in Canada. Consequently, Flowers and Smith saw no reason to move the boats on northward. It is also possible that they saw no reason to pay duty on the boats, so simply abandoned them rather than hauling them back to tidewater.

Several years ago the National Park Service very carefully assembled one of the canoes and proved they would have been of marginal value to anyone except as personal transportation on calm water.

Whatever the reasons behind their existence, most of them will remain where they were found. There is a possibility that the park service will build some kind of shelter over them so they won't disintegrate completely. Several were removed—nobody knows exactly how many—before the national park was established.

Once you reach the summit and start downhill, you will see a small portable cabin on a ledge standing above the snow. The Canadian flag will be flying over it because this is the first of several warming huts and emergency shelters placed along the trail by the Canadian Parks Service. A park warden (the U.S. park rangers' Canadian counterparts are called wardens) may be inside. As with all warming huts, hikers are not permitted to set up housekeeping in them. The huts are places to warm up, perhaps change clothes, then move on so the next hikers can use them.

In addition to the summit cabin, the Canadian Parks Service has similar shelters just below the summit at Crater Lake, Happy Camp, Deep Lake, Lake Lindeman (the park headquarters), Bare Loon Lake and Lake Bennett.

CHAPTER 6

The Summit
to Lake Bennett

The climatic difference between the Alaska side and the Canadian side of the trail is dramatic. Often when you cross the summit in fiercely blowing whiteout conditions, the sodden clouds will begin breaking up overhead and you will see sunshine ahead on Crater Lake. It is much drier on the Canadian side so the mountain scenery can be seen easily and more fully enjoyed. Three vegetation zones are found on this side of the park: the Alpine tundra and meadow, subalpine and boreal forest. More than forty species of mammals have been spotted on the Canadian side along with more than 130 species of birds.

Very often the foul weather of the summit climb will disappear before you reach Lake Lindeman. Even if you have overcast weather all the way to Lake Bennett, rainfall is infrequent below Long Lake.

The descent from the summit to Crater Lake is down a steep, permanent snowbank that will make you glad you have an alpenstock or crampons. The flagged route goes along the side of the permanent snowbank that forces you to walk downhill on snow that slopes off to the left. It is a rare hiker who doesn't slip, and falls are common. Don't try to glissade down it because you'll likely end up in a pile of boulders.

The trail takes you down to the shore of the jewel-like Crater Lake and the stone crib that was built to anchor an aerial tramway. The Canadian Parks Service has a small warming hut just below the crib on a rock outcropping. Some of the timbers holding the stones in place remain intact while others have rotted and parts of the crib have crumbled.

All around the lakeshore are signs of the stampede: a stone causeway built out to one of the little islands, an aluminum canoe crushed and abandoned beside the lake, wagon tracks and indentions on the lakeshore gravel and marsh where boats were pulled out of the water.

The route levels out immediately when you reach Crater Lake and for most of the way down to Long Lake you will walk on wet ground, sometimes in water coming over your boot tops from the snowfields above. Not far from Crater Lake you will see a low ledge with tall grass growing atop it and a scattering of rotten boards and parts of wagons. This is where a teamster built his barn, and the grass that grows there is from the hay he shipped in for his horses. Like so many entrepreneurs, he abandoned almost everything when the stampede ended rather than hauling it out. As you walk on past the site you will see ruts made by the wagons he used to haul gear from Crater Lake to the head of Long Lake, where boats could be hired to transport it to the far end just above Deep Lake. If the snow is completely gone from the valley floor, you will see the wagon tracks at intervals all the way to Long Lake. At the northern end of Long Lake you can see more causeways built out into the lake to make the transfer between boats and wagons easier.

The first place camping is permitted on the Canadian side is Happy Camp, five miles from the summit and eight miles from Sheep Camp. The rugged site, apparently named because stampeders were so happy to find a place to camp, has shelter from the wind and is on high, dry ground. However, since the site is small the best campsites are usually taken early in the afternoon and you may have to pitch your tent on rocks. The Canadian Parks Service has a shelter there that gives hikers a chance to rest and dry out before continuing the trek.

When you reach the upper end of Long Lake, the trail switchbacks up to the top of a ridge overlooking the lake, follows it to the end of the lake, then winds down to a bridge across the short, swift stream that connects Long Lake with Deep Lake, a small, picturesque lake with boulders and tiny islands dotting its surface. The camping area is at the end of the bridge and this is where the timberline reappears, mostly stunted spruce with some willow and other low brush.

The two-mile hike to Lake Lindeman is along a ridge high above the waterfalls and rapids in the stream that empties Deep Lake. Much of the trail is punctuated by exposed roots and rocks that make hiking slow and laborious, the kind where you see very little scenery because you must keep your eyes on the trail to avoid stumbling and falling. You will see an occasional collapsed cabin from the winter of 1897–1898 along the trail, and you'll also see dozens of stumps about four feet high. These stumps were left when stampeders chopped down the scrawny trees when snow was two or three feet deep, leaving stumps that look like posts for a fence built by a demented hired hand.

Lake Lindeman appears as you round a bend in the trail and begin a sudden, steep ascent. Below, you will see the older cabin built on the lake shore in the late 1960s, and straight ahead due north is the Canadian Parks Service complex of visitor center, museum, mess hall and dormitories. The valley floor is strewn with remnants of the stampede, including broken glass, so be careful where you pitch your tent and don't walk around the area barefooted, no matter how much your feet may ache from the trail. Another reminder of that long winter of 1897–1898 is a cemetery with eleven graves atop a low hill.

The Lindeman City area is flat, and you will have a wide choice of campsites beneath the trees. If you camp there overnight, you will go to sleep to the comforting sound of the wind blowing through the trees. The Canadian Parks Service has several picnic tables scattered among the trees, and the old cabin on the shore has a woodstove and tables inside and outside. Outhouses are back in the timber. The area is so inviting after the rigors of the trail that some hikers stay an extra day to rest, tend to their blisters and dry out their sleeping bags and clothing before going on the guided walking tours of Lindeman City offered by Canadian Parks Service wardens.

The remaining seven miles to Lake Bennett are almost anticlimactic after mastering the pass, but it is a pretty hike through the spruce forest, across noisy streams and along the shore of Bare Loon Lake. This lake was named by one of the first tour operators to lead hikes over Chilkoot Pass in the early 1970s. Skip Burns, owner of Klondike Safaris, and his staff of college students carried most of the hikers' equipment for them and often camped one night beside an unnamed lake between Lindeman and Bennett lakes. Sometimes they heard the cry of loons and sometimes they went skinny-dipping. Thus, Bare Loon Lake. The name stuck and appears on park service maps.

The trail forks just north of Bare Loon Lake and you have a choice of continuing on to Lake Bennett on the trail or swinging over to the White Pass and Yukon Route railroad. Some hikers feel they've seen enough and save a few miles of hiking by going directly to the railroad. A few hardy souls hike all the way out—twelve miles on the railroad right-of-way—to the highway at Fraser. They do so at their own risk and discomfort because the railroad has the right of way posted against trespassing, and backpacking on railroad ties is a form of self-flagellation.

For more than half a century the White Pass and Yukon Route trains stopped for lunch at Bennett. The passengers and crew had the family-style roast beef meal described earlier. Also the crews changed

The shell of St. Andrews Church stands at the foot of Chilkoot Trail, where it ends on the shore of Lake Bennett. The church was built during the period of heaviest use of the trail, 1898–1900. Photo by the author.

here. Americans working only between Bennett and Skagway, and the Canadians between Whitehorse and Bennett.

The most prominent landmark at Lake Bennett is the boldly designed St. Andrews Church standing on the high hill with a view north down Lake Bennett. It was started during the winter of 1898 at the instigation of Rev. Andrew S. Grant, the Presbyterian minister in Skagway who thought Bennett City would become a large and permanent settlement. His replacement, Rev. J. A. Sinclair, laid the cornerstone on May 24, 1899, and he designed the church in the Gothic Revival style so popular in the Victorian era. However, when the railroad was completed in 1900, most of the population moved away and the church had its last service in 1902. It has been protected by generations of Canadians. It recently was stabilized and portions were rebuilt by the Canadian Parks Service.

Although souvenir hunters have combed the area for artifacts over the decades, several traces of the stampeders remain. One record of their passing is the series of circular tent sites dug out of the sandy banks along the lakeshore below the church. Remains of cabins and saw pits can be seen along the river that flows in from Lake Lindeman, and various bits and pieces of sawmill equipment and boats are scattered in the timber and along the banks.

White Pass and Yukon Route runs a rail motorcar service for hikers on a twice-daily basis during the summer. Powered by an automobile engine, they are called Casey cars, and have very basic seating. The car takes you to Fraser on the Skagway–Carcross highway, which is where the Canadian customs station was built and where the tour buses meet the White Pass and Yukon Route trains that come up from Skagway.

The service has been so successful that White Pass and Yukon Route began running a train from Fraser to Bennett once a day, arriving in the late afternoon, to bring hikers out. Future plans are uncertain, but if traffic warrants it, the service will continue. Check with White Pass and Yukon Route or the National Park Service while making your plans, preferably before leaving home. (Addresses and telephone numbers are listed in the Sources of Information section of the Appendix.)

CHAPTER 7

The Headwater Lakes

If the White Pass and Yukon Route railroad resumes operations and it becomes possible to have canoes or boats dropped off at Bennett you will have two choices of boat trips to take: You can follow the exact Klondike route (Bennett–Nares–Tagish–Marsh lakes and down the river), which will be described later, or you can follow the route taken by steamboats when they cruised these lakes. These lake boats, much smaller than the river boats, met the train at Carcross. Here they loaded tourists, passengers and freight and steamed down Windy Arm to a mine, then back up and east to Taku Arm. The major stops were the Engineer Gold Mine, and Ben-My-Chree at very end of the lake near the foot of the mountains.

After Mr. and Mrs. Otto Partridge took it over they found that a combination of a micro-climate and rich soil make it a good place to plant a large flower and vegetable garden. They struck a deal with the steamboat companies to make it a tourist stop. Here passengers took a walk through the garden and were entertained by a zoo of mythological critters made of wood by Mr. Partridge, including a mosquito as large as a collie. They were served tea and crumpets, sometimes rhubarb wine, in the dining room, where businessmen added their business cards to the collection thumb-tacked to one wall.

After the Partridges died, White Pass and Yukon Route took it over, keeping the gardens neat and making tea and crumpets for the passengers. When the steamboats were replaced by the spur off the Alaska Highway to Atlin, the place was abandoned. When I was there almost exactly twenty years later, the buildings were still intact, furniture undamaged and one wall in the dining room layered with business cards.

The Classic Klondike Route

These mileages are strictly of the as-the-crow-flies variety and are based on Geographic Survey of Canada maps.

Bennett Station to Carcross	30 miles
Carcross (Nares Lake) to Windy Arm	6 miles
Windy Arm to Tagish Lake	8 miles
Tagish Lake to Marsh Lake	12 miles
Marsh Lake to Yukon River outlet	20 miles
Marsh Lake to Whitehorse	50 miles
Total from Bennett Station to Whitehorse	126 miles

Headwater Lakes Trip as Described in Text

Lake Atlin (2 x 66)	132 miles
Atlin River	2 miles
Grahame Inlet	16 miles
Taku Arm from Tagish to Grahame Inlet	20 miles
Grahame Inlet to Ben-My-Chree	18 miles
Total Lake Atlin to Whitehorse one way	188 miles

From Ben-My-Chree the steamboats went back north to Grahame Inlet and ran due east to its end at the mouth of the Atlin River. Here at a station called Taku a tiny train named the Little Dutchess pulled a string of open passenger and freight cars two miles along the river to Scotia Bay on Lake Atlin. There another steamboat, the *Tarahne*, met them and took them across the lake to the town of Atlin.

The *Tarahne* sits on the beach in Atlin and the Little Dutchess is on display in Carcross. For nearly forty years the other lake steamboat, the *Tutshi*, sat beside the Little Dutchess in Carcross, but it was virtually destroyed by a fire, as were the two beautiful river paddlewheelers that sat on the riverbank at Whitehorse.

The headwater lake trip is one of the most beautiful boat trips in the North, but since the lakes are so vast and the weather is subject to sudden changes, it is best to take a large boat with an outboard motor. When I took my family—the youngest was five—on a trip through these headwaters, we rented a twenty-six-foot freighter canoe with a twenty-horsepower motor and had it delivered from Whitehorse to Atlin.

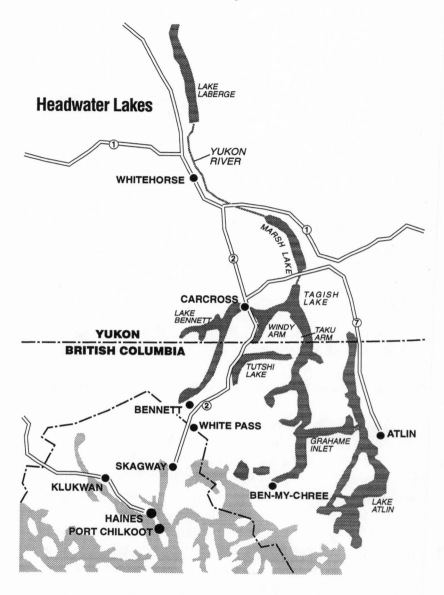

We camped three nights on islands in Lake Atlin, went to the extreme south end and hiked a trail to the snout of Llewellyn Glacier that comes down from the Juneau Icecap. We returned to Atlin to hire a guide to take us down the Atlin River. This two-mile-long river runs about ten miles an hour over rapids, around boulders, backwashes and shallows, and most of the bank is too sheer to stop and scout ahead. Once safely down into Grahame Inlet, we spent a night at the old railroad station and

The Tarahne *worked Lake Atlin for decades until the Alaska Highway was built. This small, trim boat is currently under restoration by the local historical society. Photo by the author.*

ate moose and caribou steaks given to us by the generous Atlin jet-boat operators, Joe and Carol Florence, who were tragically killed in separate plane crashes a few years later. We also spent one night in cabins built by a family of trappers who lived on Grahame Inlet for several decades.

Later we cruised down Taku Arm to the foot of the mountains, visited the remains of Ben-My-Chree, then headed due north into Tagish Lake and on down the Yukon River to Whitehorse. This trip took ten days, which permitted us to spend extra time at the more interesting sites without feeling hurried.

Assuming you want to follow only the Klondike route, if you put in at Bennett, you can follow the eastern shore of Lake Bennett to avoid the sudden strong winds that whip down from the mountains and down the West Arm. Good campsites are on the small islands that mark the British Columbia–Yukon border, on points and in sheltered coves. With train service suspended, you won't be rousted from your sleeping bag by a screaming diesel in the middle of the night.

When you reach Carcross, the route turns due east through Nares Lake, which is a cross between a lake and a lazy river because it is broad and moves slowly into Tagish. Windy Arm enters Tagish where the Nares enters the main lake, and Windy Arm earned its name from the storms that sometimes come down from the mountains and blow across the lake. Thus, it is best to stay close to the north shore of Tagish.

Tagish turns northwest where Taku Arm joins it, and a small town named Tagish grew where the lake ends and becomes a stream that feeds into Marsh Lake. Here the Alaska Highway spur to Carcross crosses a bridge while the main Alaska Highway runs down the east side of Marsh Lake on its way to Whitehorse. The bridge area is a popular place for bank fishermen.

Marsh Lake is the least attractive of the headwater lakes because it has no dramatic mountains for a backdrop, nor does it have tall timber along its shores. Nevertheless, it is a popular place for summer cabins and is so shallow that its water warms up enough for water skiers in the summer months.

The Yukon River begins without fanfare: The lake comes to a point on the north end and the water gradually begins moving out of the lake through tall grasses. One moment you are paddling to make headway and almost immediately the current catches you; then you paddle only for steerage.

The first few miles of the river are slow and the banks marshy with many sloughs and islands because of the backwaters from the Marsh Lake Dam a short distance downstream. The dam, built to help flush ice out of Lake Laberge during the steamboat years, has little use today beyond being part of a flood-control system to help adjust the height of Lake Schwatka behind the Whitehorse hydroelectric dam just below Miles Canyon. It has a self-service lock on the east side that is simple to use. Below the dam the river continues on its twisting and turning route, past homes and ranches and boat docks, more civilized than wild.

After fifty miles the river picks up speed as it nears Miles Canyon, and a warning sign is posted to alert boaters the canyon is coming up around the next bend to the right. In the event the sign is down, watch for another sign describing the site of Canyon City, and if that too is missing, keep in mind that Miles Canyon is created by the only outcropping of basalt in the area. You will see the basaltic cliffs before entering the canyon.

Stop for a look around the townsite and the few remains of the wooden tramway before going into the canyon. Although the canyon has been mostly tamed, it still can be a dangerous place if you are inexperienced or careless because the water still runs very fast through and is choppy in places. Once you are through it, the river suddenly dies in Lake Schwatka and you will have to paddle down to the large dock on the left, or west, end of the dam to take out and make the portage around the dam and spillway. You can ask around for a place to store your equipment while in Whitehorse. The Royal Canadian Mounted Police is always your best source of this kind of information, although almost anyone you meet working around the river will be able to help.

River Route from Whitehorse to Dawson City

Here are the approximate distances between major sites along the river from Whitehorse (Mile 0) to Dawson City (Mile 460).

Takhini River	15 miles
Lake Laberge	30 miles
Lower Laberge	60 miles
Hootalinqua	90 miles
Big Salmon	125 miles
Little Salmon	160 miles
Carmacks	200 miles
Five Finger Rapids	224 miles
Yukon Crossing	236 miles
Minto	258 miles
Fort Selkirk	282 miles
White River	380 miles
Stewart Island	390 miles
Dawson City	460 miles

CHAPTER 8

Whitehorse

Whitehorse is a lively and attractive city with lots of trees, and flowers in planter boxes. Here you will find practically every amenity; good hotels, outdoor gear, bank cash machines, sidewalk cafes, well-stocked grocery stores and good restaurants. Whitehorse has the lowest median age of any city in Canada—somewhere in the mid-30s—and thus the highest birth rate. It also has a large population of Quebec transplants who help keep the French language alive in the North.

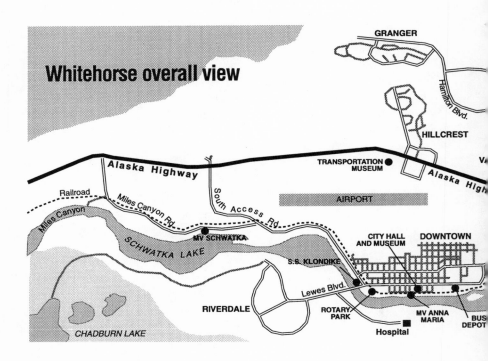

The excellent Yukon Archives are a few miles outside of town on the Yukon College campus. Here you can browse through the extensive collection of Klondike photographs, diaries and hundreds of books and pamphlets. The archives also contains a massive collection of steamboat memorabilia.

Another highlight is the steamboat *Klondike*, one of the few paddle-wheelers remaining from the fleet of more than two hundred that ran up and down the river over a period of half a century. The *Klondike* is the second to carry that name. The first was built in Whitehorse in 1929 and was the largest ever built at 210 feet long and 42 feet wide. Its cargo capacity was three hundred tons. It sank on the Thirtymile River in 1936, and the present vessel, almost an exact copy of the first, was built and launched in 1937. The paddlewheeler made the trip from Whitehorse to Dawson City in a day and a half, and from Dawson City back upriver to Whitehorse in two to five days, depending on the load and the number of times the crew had to climb overboard into the swift, cold water to haul a cable ashore so it could winch itself off a gravel bar.

The *Klondike* served as an ore and general cargo carrier between Dawson City and Mayo until the highway was opened in 1952. It ran another three years as a tourist boat but there wasn't enough business to support it, so it went onto the beach forever.

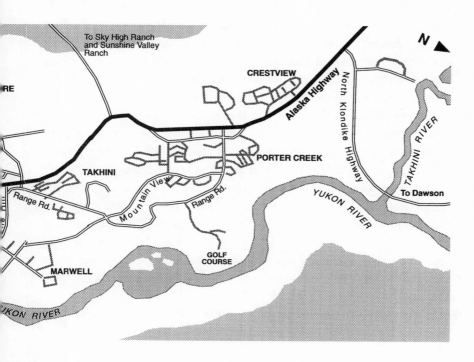

CHAPTER 9

Whitehorse
to Lake Laberge

Although it isn't required, it is a good idea to register with the Mounties in Whitehorse and tell them where you are going and your approximate arrival date. You can also buy fishing licenses at the Mountie office and check on river conditions. And when you arrive in Dawson City, please remember to tell the Mounties that you have arrived.

Most boaters going downriver put in at the boat launch in Rotary Park, just off Second Avenue near the Klondike. Some put in behind the White Pass and Yukon Route depot at the foot of Main Street but it is more difficult. The major canoe rental company, The Kanoe People, has its office a short distance downstream from the foot of Main Street, and you can buy copies of the two books of river maps and local lore from them. They are perhaps the best source of information about the river because they are in constant contact with their customers and other boaters.

From Whitehorse downriver the Yukon is polluted, so you must purify your drinking water. This includes water taken from streams entering the river due to the presence of ghardia, also known as beaver fever. Chemically treat all water or boil it at least ten minutes.

Lake Laberge is thirty miles from Whitehorse, which is about the right distance for the first day's paddling. Unless you leave late in the day, you should be able to camp somewhere on the shore of Lake Laberge that evening. The river above the lake curves gently and has many cutbanks with sweepers, which are undercut trees that lean out over the water ready to fall into the river with the next high-water period. Avoid them because they can easily "sweep" your canoe or kayak.

As you enter Lake Laberge you will see a row of piling stretching off to the left, or north. This was an ingenious attempt to direct the flow

An old steamboat navigational aid on Lake Laberge. Photo by the author.

of the river so the current would keep the lake entrance cleared of the heavy load of silt that settles to the bottom as soon as the current slows. However, the shallow bottom in the entrance has little or no effect on canoes, kayaks or small boats.

As noted earlier, the lake was named for Michael Laberge, a French-Canadian who went north to work for the Western Union Telegraph Company in 1865. The company planned to build an overland telegraph line to St. Michael, then run it underwater to Russia and on into Europe. When the trans-Atlantic cable was successfully laid, Western Union abandoned the project and Laberge stayed in the North, first as a partner in the Pioneer American Fur Company in Alaska, then as an employee of the Alaska Commercial Company. He retired in 1875 and returned to Quebec. Oddly, he never saw the lake that bears his name.

Lake Laberge is at just the right distance from the St. Elias Range to the west to be in the path of weather systems that cause it to be subject to sudden and violent weather changes. It is wise to stay close to the eastern shore, where you can find shelter and good landing places quickly. The shore has tons of wood suitable for campfires, and small, pleasant coves sheltered from the weather by trees and boulders that offer protection from the wind and waves.

A large island is about one-fourth way down the lake, and is named Richtofen Island. When the steamboat companies were in business they

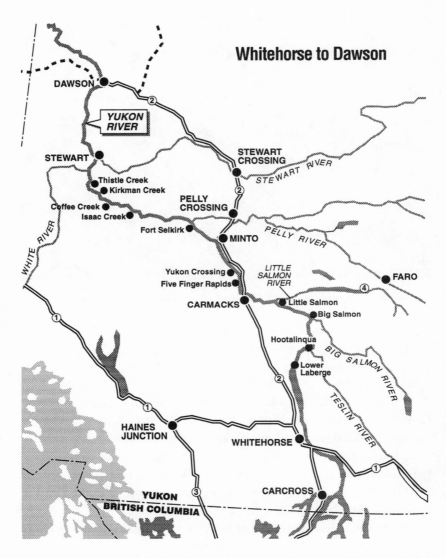

Whitehorse to Dawson

had crews staying on Richtofen in the spring when ice still covered the lake. The crews spread a 30-mile-long trail of black soot, oil and ashes down the lake to speed the thawing. A train caboose and a bunkhouse–cookshack were placed on the southern end of the island, and remains of them can still be seen there. Some people launch their boats or canoes at the Deep Creek government campground on the western side of the lake opposite Richtofen Island, then camp on the island because it is beautiful with high plateaus and sheltered coves. However, locals recommend that you stay on the eastern shore for safety from the weather. The eastern shoreline has numerous sheltered coves and pebbled beaches, and tons of firewood have washed ashore over the decades.

Nearly every day a storm blows across Lake Laberge, so it is difficult to predict how long it will take you to paddle its length. Some are able to leave Whitehorse in the morning and camp that night on the lower end of Laberge, but it isn't unusual to spend two or three days making that initial sixty miles.

After having to paddle thirty miles, Lower Laberge is a welcome sight. A reef is in the middle of the entrance to the river, often covered during the spring high-water periods and exposed from about July onward. To the right is the skeleton of the steamboat *Casca*, which loses a little more of its wooden framework each year. Originally, Lower Laberge was a large town with two dozen cabins. It was a major way station for the steamboats, and later the horse- and tractor-powered sleighs that went over the old winter road between Dawson City and Whitehorse. A Mountie post stood across the river and a woodcutter's camp was nearby; after fighting their way up the swift and dangerous Thirtymile River, the paddlewheelers always needed to replenish their wood supply before going on the last leg of the journey to Whitehorse.

Lower Laberge also had a telegraph station that was part of the system that ran along the river and was used from 1899 until the telephone system was installed along the highway in the 1950s. Although following the river wasn't necessarily the shortest route, it was the most convenient for patrolling the line; a few remnants of line can still be seen, but most of the insulators have been taken by tourists. The system was a descendant of two failed telegraph lines. The first was begun by an under-financed group in 1857 that hoped to capitalize on the problems of the trans-Atlantic line, which had recently broken. They planned to go from the Vancouver area north to the Yukon River and follow it into Alaska, which then was still Russian America, then cross the Bering Sea into Russia and Europe. They reached Fort St. Michael in July 1867, celebrated by drinking from insulators and firing their blunderbusses, then learned that the new Atlantic cable had been in operation a year.

Much of the system did get built, though, and finally was put into operation in 1901 when two crews going in opposite directions met north of Hazelton, British Columbia, but only after somebody discovered that the crews had bypassed each other by several miles.

Men were stationed about every fifty miles to keep the system functioning, no matter the weather. There were cases of these solitary men becoming seriously ill, injuring themselves or even accidentally shooting themselves while the other operators sat by their set, listening for the electrical impulses that would tell them if the operator was still alive. After being on the job a few months, the operators could tell who was sending the Morse code signals by the way the operator touched the key.

With so much time on their hands they could dream up many ways to amuse themselves. One operator had unexpected company for several days when a family stopped by and their horses took off while they were visiting. The family stayed long enough for the operator to fall in love with the daughter. After riding the sixty-five miles to visit her, then back again, the operator came up with a better solution: He moved his station, which was no more difficult than splicing his sending and receiving set into the telegraph wire. He built himself a crude shack near the girl's home and continued the courtship. Someone told the company about the romance and the love-stricken operator soon had orders to pack up his equipment and march back down the trail to the original station.

There were also the inevitable practical jokers. One operator waited until one of the coldest nights of the year to wake all his peers and tell them to go out and see a perfect moon eclipse. All along the route, for more than one thousand miles, men hurriedly slipped on their winter clothes and went outside to see a perfect full moon. One can only guess at the messages tapped out to the perpetrator when they went back inside.

It is little wonder they dreamed up practical jokes, for they had one of the most lonely jobs imaginable. They had to stay at their posts for two years before they could take a two-month leave, and sometimes their only human contact was the morning roll call the company imposed to be sure all men were still at their posts and not ill, injured or dead. The former telegraph cabin at Lower Laberge has been used during the winters by a trapper for a number of years and he has placed a guest book inside that carries names and comments from residents of virtually every country in Europe and many around the Pacific Rim.

The townsite also has a shelter for camping and cooking, but the best camping is on the exposed gravel bar beside the river; the Lower Laberge mosquitoes are so aggressive in the sheltered areas that they could well be a separate species. The same might be said for the ground squirrels—they show no fear of mankind and will steal anything they can carry away, including parts of your lunch while you are eating it.

CHAPTER 10

The Thirtymile River

The Thirtymile River is nearly everyone's favorite stretch of the Yukon. The water that emerges from Lake Laberge is the clearest you will see on the trip. But don't drink it untreated. The Thirtymile River is also swift: It twists and turns as gracefully as a Viennese waltz the whole thirty miles to Hootalinqua. The channel is narrow and bordered by cutbanks, low banks with tall stands of timber and wind-carved cliffs with gargoyle-like protrusions of sandstone. The river has no rapids and the worst of the rocks were dynamited out by the steamboat companies, but it does have a few backwashes and small eddies to keep it interesting for paddlers.

Numerous bald eagles cruise the river for salmon and other fish, and you'll occasionally see a black bear or grizzly bear, sometimes a moose. Here, you will also find the best fishing on the main river, because it is so clear. Elsewhere, you will have to fish only where clear streams enter the lakes or river.

Although the river presents virtually no danger for canoes or small boats, the narrow, swift and rock-filled Thirtymile was dreaded by steamboaters and it cost more lives and property damage than any other part of the river system. During the 1898 stampede more outfits were lost on it than in Miles Canyon, in part because dire warnings were not issued about it. Numerous photographs from the stampede show people standing on shore, drenched and forlorn with their boat or raft demolished.

Many of the rocks, bends and creeks were named for vessels wrecked on or near them, the skippers of steamboats who hit them or people who drowned: Casey Rock, Domville Creek, Casca Reef, Tanana Reef. In recent years, scuba divers have been exploring the riverbottom in search of the wrecked steamboats and an inventory and map of them is being compiled.

Thirtymile River

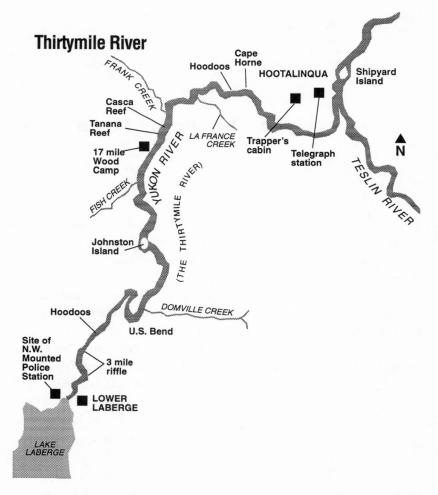

The Thirtymile has been added to the Canadian Heritage Rivers System because of its beauty and these characteristics:

It has the clearest water of the Yukon River, which makes it important to salmon migration.

It has interesting exposures of white volcanic ash along the bank that was deposited more than twelve hundred years ago.

It has several examples of moraines, eskers and other evidence of glaciation.

It has deeply incised tributary channels, slumping and undercut river banks, almost perpendicular sand and gravel bluffs one hundred feet high, hoodoos and constantly changing gravel bars.

Hootalinqua, Yukon River. Photo by the author.

The shorelines and islands are covered in subarctic forests of aspen, birch, poplar and large mature stands of pine and spruce, which makes it excellent habitat for muskrat, beaver, weasel, red fox, lynx, coyote, wolf, mink and black bear.

It supports the endangered wolverine and the rare grizzly bear, bald and golden eagles, trumpeter swans, migratory waterfowl, bank swallows and diving ducks.

A scattering of primitive campsites have been built along the river, including one on the downstream tip of Johnson Island that is one of the prettiest campsites on the entire Yukon River. The river valley is a good place for hiking, and the surrounding low hills are good places for photographing the river.

It is about the only stretch of open river that is good for fishing and you can expect to catch grayling, salmon (in season), pike, lake trout, whitefish and inconnu. You must have a territorial fishing license.

The river ends when it joins the Teslin River at Hootalinqua. This townsite is a pretty place to camp and has two or three buildings remaining from the steamboat days. Camping is spread out from an open area at the boat landing back into the timber and beside a clear, swift stream. The view is across the Yukon and up the Teslin with low mountains behind it.

161

CHAPTER 11

Hootalinqua to Carmacks

N o more than one hundred yards below Hootalinqua is an island that is known as Shipyard Island. Steamboats were stored here during the winter, and hauled up for repairs at other times. Along the way is the slowly rotting remains of a paddlewheeler named at various times the *Evelyn* or the *Norcam*. It was in service from 1908 until 1931, then retired and stored on the island for spare parts and perhaps as a workshop and bunkhouse. The island also has good camp sites, but no fresh water.

The Teslin River brings a load of silt into the Yukon, and the clear water of the Thirtymile River is no more. The Yukon is opaque from Hootalinqua to the sea. It also slows considerably below Hootalinqua, although it still flows between five and ten miles an hour, fast enough for paddlers to lie back and enjoy the scenery while making only an occasional dip of the paddle for steerage or to avoid a riffle or debris in the water. Early in the season when the water is running high, you will share the river with trees, stumps and assorted debris. Occasionally, as you pass cutbanks, you will be treated to the sight of minor landslides as the loose dirt gives way and a sheet of soil cascades into the river.

Although you will pass an occasional abandoned woodcamp or cabin, the next village of any significance is Big Salmon, where the river of the same name enters. The site was used by natives for centuries, and when the Klondike stampede occurred, the Mounties built a post and a telegraph station across the river from the village, parts of which still stand. A few buildings from the village remain, and the bank exposed to the weather makes it a good place to camp if the wind is blowing to keep the mosquitoes away.

Not far below Big Salmon on the right, or east, side of the river is a dredge that has been grounded there since 1940. It was built by

Native American cemetery at Little Salmon, on the Yukon River. Note the wooden spirit houses in the background. Photo by the author.

Lawrence Cyr and Boyd Gordon and first used on the Takhini River. The owners were working their way down the river, dredging here and there, when winter caught them at the base of the bluff. They were getting enough gold to keep it operating but not much more. With winter coming, they dug a place for it in the bank and went to White-horse. They reportedly had a disagreement that winter and they never returned to move it.

Little Salmon is the next village, and it has one of the largest and best-tended Native American cemeteries along the river. No buildings survived but the large cemetery has been surrounded by a painted fence, and the spirit houses that were built over many of the graves have been repaired and painted.

As an aside, spirit houses are a fixture through much of the Yukon. According to the writer/photographer Richard Harrington, these miniature houses resulted not from some spiritual experience but from clever merchandising by sawmill owners after the gold rush and its building boom ended. These salesmen were quite successful with the idea of placing houses to protect the graves and the items buried with the owner. They were quickly named spirit houses and were equipped with real doors and windows and scaled down furniture. Mourners placed favorite toys, tools, photos and other items in them.

163

No campsites exist around the Little Salmon townsite, and residents suggest that visitors first go downstream a short distance to the landing where a few people live and ask permission to visit the cemetery before tramping through it.

Carmacks is next, the only real town on the river and the only place you will cross the Klondike Highway, although you will see it from time to time before Carmacks and again downstream near Five Finger Rapids. Carmacks was obviously named to honor the discoverer of the Klondike gold because he had lived in the area before going downriver and had operated a trading post and the Tantalus Butte coal mine just upriver from town. You can see the mine high on the hill, a dark hole in the granite butte.

Carmacks is the only place you can stock up on food and other supplies, including gasoline, so you will most likely stop here. Be prepared—the river is very swift and you should be near the left bank before going under the bridge so you can be prepared for the landing at the large government campground almost directly below the highway bridge. The campground has firepits with wood provided, toilets, a picnic shelter and fresh water at the pump. Unfortunately, the campground is also directly beneath the elevated highway over which heavy trucks roar day and night, and it is also a popular place for local youths to party through the night.

If you can arrive early in the day, you might consider doing your shopping, having a restaurant meal if you want, then go back on the river to camp downstream. If you don't plan to stay long, you can also tie up at the foot of the main road that leads up to the stores along the highway. It is a short walk from the river to the stores, no more than two city blocks.

Perhaps a fourth of the people who go down the Yukon end their trip at Carmacks. It makes a good five- or six-day trip from Whitehorse because it is roughly two hundred miles by river and only a two-hour drive, so it is easy to drop a car there for the return trip.

CHAPTER 12

Carmacks to Fort Selkirk

It is twenty-four miles from Carmacks to Five Finger Rapids, and you will pass several fish camps along this stretch of river. Most belong to Native Americans who use nets to catch the salmon that have migrated more than two thousand miles from the Bering Sea. In late summer the camps will have racks covered with salmon laid out to dry.

It isn't necessary to scout Five Finger Rapids because there are only one or two bumps and you're through them. The best channel is the same one used by the steamboats, the one farthest to the right between the shore and the first flowerpot island that makes up the "fingers." If you have your canoe pointed directly into the standing wave, you should have no problem, although there's a good chance everyone will get wet. Once past the standing wave, stay right and go on the right side of the island directly below the rapids. This channel will take you to the small camp and territorial park at Tachun Creek, where you can dry out, have lunch and find some shelter.

Rink Rapids is four miles below Tachun Creek, and they present even less danger than Five Finger Rapids. You can miss most of the fun by staying close to the right, or eastern, shore. Originally Rink Rapids was very rough but the steamboat companies dropped several tons of dynamite behind the rocks that created the rapids and reduced most of them to gravel.

From here to Fort Selkirk, another fifty-four miles, the river broadens and is cluttered with islands of all sizes. Camping is good on those that have broad, open areas, and you'll also find good sites on the bank. Unless there are a lot of people on the river, you can usually find a campsite at one of the old towns or trapper's cabin with large, cleared

Five Finger Rapids is where the Yukon River takes the shape of an outstretched hand, pointing toward the gold fields. Sternwheelers, during and after the gold rush, had to be winched through these rapids. Photo courtesy Tourism Yukon.

areas in front and good places to beach your canoe or boat. As with everywhere in the North, the key is an open area where the breezes can blow away the mosquitoes. Although it is best not to camp in the empty cabins along the river, should you choose to do so, it is a good idea to take along mosquito coils, those small smudge-pot gadgets that discourage mosquitoes.

Minto is the next stop, a small town just off the highway. In case of an emergency, or if you find yourself fed up with the river or your traveling companions, this is your last chance to leave the river. Minto has a motel with a dining room, but at this writing it was used only for bus tour groups. But the resort does have a bathhouse and laundry, which river travelers can use at a modest cost.

It is only twenty-four miles from Minto to Fort Selkirk and many travelers stop here for an extra day to laze around, get the kinks out of their backs and putter around the large ghost town. It is a welcome sight for river travelers when the long shelf opposite the Pelly River appears with its collection of buildings lining the bank like elderly soldiers on parade. Perhaps a dozen buildings are in the town, including a church, store, school, several cabins and an interpretative center at the upstream end of town. A deep notch down to the water was cut in the bank decades ago so carts could be wheeled to and from the steamboats. Most canoes land at this spot, although another landing with wooden steps was built slightly upstream. The force of the Pelly River keeps the current pushed against the bank and the river runs very swift here, making paddlers dig in for a few strokes.

The village has a caretaker, who meets all visitors with a guest book, and who will help you get a wood supply for the firepits that have been dug around the camp area. Back in the timber is a large cemetery, a church and spirit houses with elaborate fences. The number of graves attest to the size and importance of Fort Selkirk during the first fifty years of this century. The fort had lain abandoned after the Chilkats pillaged it and burned it in 1853. It was revived in 1889 by the trader Arthur Harper, who called it Fort Campbell.

Then it became headquarters for the Yukon Field Force, the Canadian Army group sent to the Yukon during the gold rush to add weight to Canada's claim on the area. A detachment of Mounties was stationed there and the Anglican Church had a mission school. When the Klondike Highway was completed and the steamboats stopped running, the town was abandoned almost overnight.

The far side of the river has basalt palisades about fifty feet high. This rusty iron and black mass begins up the Pelly River a few miles and curves around into the Yukon, forming a solid wall that continues downriver more than twenty miles. It ends abruptly when the basalt disappears into the face of a hillside.

CHAPTER 13

Fort Selkirk
to Dawson City

The character of the river changes below Selkirk. The forest becomes thicker and the undergrowth more dense. Although the river doesn't narrow, the high hills and bluffs along it make the river valley seem almost claustrophobic at times. Although the short growing season and severe winters keep the trees from growing rapidly, the wetter climate makes the underbrush—and the mosquitoes—grow thick and healthy. If you are lucky enough to find a barren sandbar for a campsite toward the end of the day, you'd better take it rather than waiting until "the next one," because it might be several miles away.

A number of creeks enter the river along this stretch, and each has been or is inhabited. Each has a story about people who have lived there, often eccentric folk or at the least very independent. These creeks were the site of cabins built by trappers, prospectors, woodcutters, trappers and other loners. Some of the cabins are back in use today, at least on a seasonal basis, and most owners have dogs to alert them of visitors. Common courtesy requires you to announce your presence by shouting a hello or two from the bank before proceeding to the cabin. It is also a good opportunity to inquire about campsites down the river.

Although the river is lacking in whitewater, it does have its moments of intense interest, and one is where the White River enters. The White comes out of the St. Elias Range and carries a heavy load of silt that is mostly volcanic ash. When it enters the Yukon it immediately turns the river into a milky color. At the confluence the white water comes roiling upward in many places, looking almost like a fountain or spring as it mixes the milky water with the more prosaic muddy water of the main river.

The next place of interest is Stewart Island, which once was quite large and had a town when gold was being mined up the Stewart River.

Dawson City as it looks today. Its population is now about 800 people, compared to over 35,000 during the gold rush. Photo courtesy Tourism Yukon.

The river was also the main avenue from the silver mines around Mayo, Elsa and Keno, but the highway put an end to that in the 1950s. Everybody moved away except the Burian family, who kept a small store and some rental cabins. The island gets smaller each year as the river eats away at it. The first time I visited it in the early 1970s we made a more or less controlled landing in an inflatable boat. When I was struggling to climb onto the bank, I looked up and saw potatoes hanging from the bank that had an overhang. The river had eaten away several feet of the garden during the night, leaving some of the potato plants dangling from the dirt that hadn't fallen in yet.

At this writing it isn't known if the Burian family will remain on the island full time because Rudy, the patriarch, died, and only Yvonne and one or two of the adult children were staying on the diminishing island.

It is seventy miles from Stewart Island to Dawson City, and a few good campsites can be found on barren islands or sandbars. The river is wide the rest of the way into Dawson City and has few points interest. Most travelers are looking forward to arriving in Dawson City and tend to rush through these last miles anyway. More and more cabins can be seen back in the timber and along the creeks because the river above Dawson City is becoming almost a suburb. An occasional small farm or truck garden is seen, and usually you'll see residents running back and forth in their motorboats.

Then you round a long bend in the river and ahead on the right is the enormous scar of the landslide that identifies Dawson City. It is still several miles away when you first see it and you have to cross the mouth of the Klondike River before pulling into the dock just below the steamboat *Keno*. As the Klondike sweeps out into the Yukon it creates an eddy which makes it easy to land at the public dock, which you'll share with the tour boat, *Yukon Lou*, several other boats and perhaps a float-plane or two.

You've arrived in Dawson City.

CHAPTER 14

The Klondike

Like one definition of a ghost town, Dawson City is a shadow of its former self. It is one of those towns that has survived and grown by capitalizing on its past. Without its history as a selling point, the town would probably exist but only because it is on the highway that connects Whitehorse and Fairbanks, Alaska.

In 1952, the local citizens formed the Klondike Visitors Association, and the organization struggled along with virtually no funds until the federal government gave them permission to build Diamond Tooth Gertie's, Canada's only legalized gambling hall. The federal government also worked with them by restoring many of the downtown buildings and building replicas of others. Arizona Charlie Meadows' Palace Grand Theater was rebuilt by the Canadian Parks Service at a cost of $300,000. The Post Office was restored and so was the steamboat *Keno*, which sits in the heart of town overlooking the river. Nearly all buildings in the downtown area have been repaired and given coats of paint. Most new buildings were designed with a turn-of-the-century theme.

Until the early 1960s, when the restoration work began, many of the stores, hotels and other public buildings were ignored. They were built on the permafrost, which thaws slightly each summer. A disquieting side effect of this thawing and freezing is that buildings sitting directly on it begin tilting and leaning wildly. Residents have since learned to build new buildings on gravel pads.

One of the strangest stories related to a building is that of the Jack London cabin. The cabin is not native to Dawson City; it was the one he lived in during the winter of 1897–1898 out on Henderson Creek. Just after he turned twenty-two, London wrote his name on the back wall of the shack, referring to himself as "miner, author," and dated it

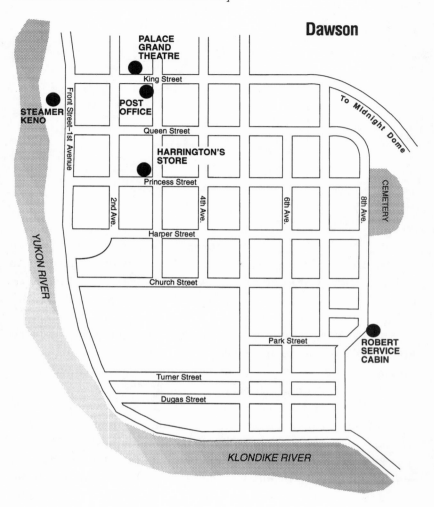

January 27, 1898. He had not found a bit of gold on the remote creek and wouldn't. Instead, he returned to Oakland, California, the following summer and began writing the string of best-selling novels and stories—*The Call of the Wild* and *White Fang* among them, plus one of his greatest short stories, "To Build a Fire," which was set on Henderson Creek.

The shack lay abandoned, the roof collapsed and it was saved only when two trappers decided to rebuild it to use as a turn-around point on their trap line. They replaced the roof, and while doing so one discovered the writing on the back wall log. Later the trappers dissolved their partnership and abandoned the cabin, but one, Jack Mackenzie, went

Dawson City, showing the Canadian Bank of Commerce, general store, and steamship Keno, *in background. Photo by the author.*

back and cut out the signature on the back wall and eventually gave it to Sam Wood, the mining recorder in Mayo who was an avid collector.

Two decades went by before anything else happened. Dick North, then a reporter for the Alaska *Daily Empire* and historian, was interviewing the Burian family on Stewart Island about Jack London because he had lived on the island. During the interview the Burians told North about the cabin. North talked to Roy Minter, director of public relations for the White Pass and Yukon Route, and Minter put up the money for North to search for the cabin.

North went to Dawson City the next spring and hired a dog team to take him the seventy-five miles to the cabin. The search party was led by a Native American named Joe Henry. His son and Robin Burian, son of Rudy and Yvonne, mushed the dogs while North followed on snowshoes. They easily found the cabin and North confirmed it by the missing piece of a log on the back wall. Next North looked up the widow of Sam Woods, who told him the piece of wood was still in her attic in Mayo. She asked a friend to photograph it for her and sent the photo to North. He showed it to handwriting experts who authenticated the signature as that of Jack London.

When the story of the cabin was printed in newspapers across North America, the Jack London Square Merchants Association in Oakland,

California, offered to raise funds to restore the cabin and move it out of the wilderness, preferably to Oakland. The Yukoners readily agreed and struck an agreement with the Californians: They would divide the cabin in half and use the logs from the upper rung going to one cabin and the lower rung to the other cabin. The Burian family dismantled the cabin and took it down to Stewart Island and built two cabins, numbering the logs, then dismantled them and took them downriver to Dawson City in their freight boat. Dawson City took one cabin and the other was taken to Oakland and reconstructed in Jack London Square by Robin Burian, Joe Henry and Dick North.

Another important factor in Dawson City's survival, indeed its rebirth, was the change in the way countries treated the gold supply. Most countries began reducing their control over the price of gold in 1967 and the result was a skyrocketing of prices that made it profitable for miners to begin working the claims along the Klondike creeks. The miners brought in bulldozers that could break up the permafrost, rubber-tired loaders, high-pressure water hoses, dump trucks and sophisticated sluice systems. Gold mining became big business again, and in 1990 the two hundred-odd placer mines were contributing some $40 million to the local economy.

CHAPTER 15

The Sourtoe Cocktail

From its very origin Dawson City has nurtured its reputation as a haven for professional characters and eccentrics, beginning with Swiftwater Bill Gates and the other original miners. It is a tradition that has carried on down to the present. The wooden and pressed-tin city has always had its share of braggarts and heroes, gentlemen and scoundrels, prostitutes and women of towering virtue, although today there are precious few, if any, of the former and many of the latter. Individuality has flourished and has been encouraged, like the cucumbers and cabbages that grow to gigantic proportions in the rich soil beneath the midnight sun.

During the 1970s and into the 1990s, one of Dawson City's most colorful, irreverent and basically decent characters has been Captain Dick Stevenson. When you first meet the captain, you may find it hard to believe that this calm, soft-spoken man is the same one who founded the Yukon Order of the Sourtoe Cocktail, the most outrageous organization in a place where outrageousness helps get citizens through the six-month winter. But when you see the gold nugget embedded in his front tooth and that gleam in his eye you begin to understand.

In addition to operating Dawson City's major tour boat, the *Yukon Lou*, Dick Stevenson has a pickled, well-formed human toe in a small, padded case. Each evening during the summer tourist season Stevenson can be found sitting quietly at the corner table of the Westmark Hotel's Keno Lounge with a drink, the toe, a membership register and a sheaf of certificates.

For $5 you can receive a Sourtoe Certificate signed by Captain Dick Stevenson. But you must earn it: First you must order a drink of your choice, straight gin or vodka are favorites, into which Stevenson drops the dismembered toe. If you can drink the whole drink, nonstop, with the toe touching your lips, you have earned a signed certificate and a round of applause.

Disgusting? Sickening? Absolutely. Yet by the end of the summer of 1991, on September 10 to be exact, 9,628 men and women had earned a certificate.

One thing more; the 1991 vintage toe he was using as this is being written is the eighth he's used so far. This exercise in control of the gag reflex began in the summer of 1973 during a long evening in the Sluice Box Lounge of the Eldorado Hotel in Dawson City. Stevenson was drinking with two of Canada's most imaginative writers, Don Sawatsky, most recently a columnist for a Whitehorse newspaper, and Dennis Bell, then a reporter for Canadian Press. Bell made one or two trips to the Yukon each year from his office in Vancouver, and invariably he found at least one hilarious story that was printed all over Canada, and sometimes all over the world. The whole territory still talks about his story that made a parrot in Carcross the most famous bird in the world. A year later the old, grouchy and foul-mouthed parrot died and it was given a state funeral that became an international event. During all those years Sawatsky was working for the territorial tourism department, taking visiting journalists on trips through the territory.

In the case of the toe, Bell and Sawatsky indulged in a bit of creative journalism and invented a better story than they had been able to find. While they drank and talked, Stevenson told them he had recently bought a cabin from an elderly man confined to the local nursing home. Included in the purchase was most of the cabin's contents, including the toe. It had belonged to the man's brother and was the result of an accident; they were bootleggers and one of the brothers got his feet wet during a winter run. Thinking the Mounties were chasing them, they kept running. The foot froze, gangrene set in and the toe had to be amputated. It isn't absolutely clear, but one version of the event has the owner of the toe swinging the hatchet.

Whatever the circumstances, it was placed in a pickle jar filled alcohol and left there, apparently forgotten. Stevenson found the toe in the jar while cleaning the cabin. The liquor had evaporated and Stevenson said the toe was "completely dried out, dark brown and as hard as a rock." Bell wrote that it looked like a gherkin.

That was the year Bell taught a bartender to make Harvey Wallbangers his way and at his price. With their minds thus lubricated, he and Sawatsky started tossing ideas around. Robert Service's poetry is sacred in the Yukon and everyone knows the one about the man forced to drink an ice-worm cocktail. Also, to become a sourdough, you must spend an entire winter in

Captain Dick Stevenson, operator of the Yukon Lou *and founder of the Yukon Order of the Sourtoe Cocktail. Photo by the author.*

the Yukon. With this catechism to work from, they soon had the basic rules established for the Yukon Order of the Sourtoe Cocktail: The participant must order a beer glass filled with champagne, drop the toe in and drink the whole glass nonstop until the toe touched the lips.

Stevenson liked the rules so much that he wrote a poem:

You can drink it fast
You can drink it slow,
But the lips have gotta touch the toe.

The Sourtoe was an immediate success. Several local people became the first members, followed by a few tourists. Then a German film company filmed people enjoying the Sourtoe Cocktail (they also filmed Stevenson's first and only nude beauty contest, but that's another story in the Dick Stevenson collection). As a result of the German filming, Stevenson found himself famous in much of Europe but unknown in Canada. That would never do, so he went to work promoting himself and Bell wrote a widely published story about the Sourtoe.

Two years later Stevenson was surprised to find that elderly ladies were climbing off tour buses and heading right for his corner table in the Eldorado. With so many seniors wanting to join, he had to change the rules. The ladies were having trouble chug-alugging an entire beer glass full of champagne, so he let people do it with the drink of their choice.

Disaster struck in 1980. A local miner was trying to set a record for the number of Sourtoe Cocktails consumed at one sitting. On the thirteenth glass, big Gary Younger swallowed the toe. Stevenson was distraught. He never expected this to occur and was totally unprepared. Would a noble organization with 725 members die from one bungled gulp? What to do, what to do?

Stevenson launched a media blitz—not to lament the loss of the toe but to find a replacement. A woman in Fort Saskatchewan, Alberta, stepped (or limped) forward and donated a toe she had lost several years earlier due to an inoperable corn. The introduction of Sourtoe No. 2 was set for June 1981, and the owner and her husband came to witness its new life.

Only a month later that disaster struck again. The Sluice Box was being renovated and somehow the toe was lost. No replacement was forthcoming, so in desperation Stevenson came up with something even more grotesque: He found a preserved testicle and penis bone from a black bear, named it the "Better Bitter Bear Ball Highball." Tourists drank that concoction with gusto too, but everyone was relieved when another toe, the victim of a power lawnmower, appeared in the mail.

The saga of the toes continued as others were lost or swallowed. A Canadian Army detachment stole one, but a woman told Stevenson she had overheard the soldiers joking about stealing the toe. Stevenson wrote a strongly worded letter to the commanding officer, who was not amused. The toe came home. Then a woman jokingly told a baseball player from the Arctic town of Inuvik that he was supposed to swallow the toe, so he did. Another was stolen from a bar where Stevenson had set up his operation on a road trip, and he was amused listening to the

Mountie explain the theft to the duty sergeant, who had never heard of the Sourtoe. Thus, by the summer of 1991 he was on his eighth toe.

Stevenson is proud of the one nonhuman member of his order. An elderly parrot named Waldo was brought in and he drank a one-ounce White Russian. His beak touched the toe and he got his certificate.

In 1990, Stevenson had to move his headquarters from the Eldorado Hotel to the Westmark after he lost a battle with a musician whose music was so loud that Stevenson's soft voice disappeared and so did most of his clients. Stevenson said that the moment a tour bus unloaded, the music started and tourists ran for cover. Fortunately, the Westmark welcomed him and his toe.

He is an accomplished promoter and beloved by newspapers, television and radio. In his autobiography, *The Saga of the Sourtoe*, Stevenson tells how he learned a valuable lesson about promotion. Not long after he moved to Western Canada from New Brunswick, he inherited $19,000 and bought a fishing camp on a lake. In three years he was flat broke. He said he had everything he needed except customers and he vowed to never let that happen again. He became adept at getting publicity; few people in Canada are better at it.

He bought a tour boat to run on the Yukon River between Dawson City and the abandoned village of Moosehide, and he added a salmon barbecue on an island just below the village. Soon he was one of the major tour operators in Dawson City. Saying he was no good at business, he eventually sold the boat and his salmon barbecue establishment on Moosehide Island (he renamed it Pleasure Island not long after he sponsored the first nude beauty contest to be held in the Yukon). Each summer he is back running the 40-foot *Yukon Lou* tour boat during the day. Each evening he can be found at the corner table in the Keno Lounge with his new English-born wife, Ann, the certificates, membership registry and pickled toe.

Waiting.

CHAPTER 16

Klondike Historic Sites

Another cabin of importance is the one Robert Service lived in from 1909 until 1912. When he moved to Dawson City, Service was already a widely published poet and was able to leave his job as a bank clerk forever. While living in the modest cabin he wrote his novel, *The Trail of Ninety-Eight*, and wrote the final volume of Yukon poems, *Songs of a Rolling Stone*. The cabin is on the eastern end of town and has been restored to the period when Service lived there. Daily readings of his poetry are given by professional actors in the yard during the summer months.

The town's major museum, the Dawson City Museum, is in the former Territorial Administration Building at Fifth and Church. The museum houses more than thirty thousand artifacts from the gold rush, plus extensive exhibits on the local Han tribe, and films and slide shows.

Other Klondike National Historic Sites are:

Dredge No. 4. Located 10 miles from town on Bonanza Creek Road, this is the largest wooden-hull dredge in North America.

Bear Creek–Gold Dredge Support Camp. This shop complex and small town that covers sixty-two acres was built to support the gold dredges, and was used until 1966. It had the most complete blacksmith and machine shops north of Vancouver.

Ft. Herchmer Tour. This group of buildings in Dawson City include the Northwest Mounted Police barracks and administrative building. Free tours daily in the summer.

After the initial gold rush, the Klondike gold fields were gradually taken over by syndicates, and enormous dredges were used to extract the gold. This photo shows the tailings left behind by one of the dredges. Photo by the author.

Harrington's Store. This building at Third Avenue and Princess Street is used for a free Canadian Parks Service photo exhibit called "Dawson as They Saw It."

The Palace Grand Theater. In addition to performances, free guided tours are offered daily in this replica of the theater at Third Avenue and King Street built by Arizona Charlie Meadows and opened in 1899.

1901 Post Office. Across the street from the Palace Grand is the restored post office where you can buy historic and collectors' stamps.

Dawson City is served by airlines, most of which fly small, propeller aircraft. At least one bus company has thrice-weekly service between Dawson City and Whitehorse, and others have routes over into Alaska. During the summer, Holland America runs a tour boat between Dawson City and Eagle, Alaska, and Captain Dick Stevenson of Sourtoe Cocktail fame operates his tour boat, *Yukon Lou*, between Dawson City and Moosehide.

Guided tours of the town and gold fields are available, and the Klondike Visitors Association offers free walking tours of the city. The

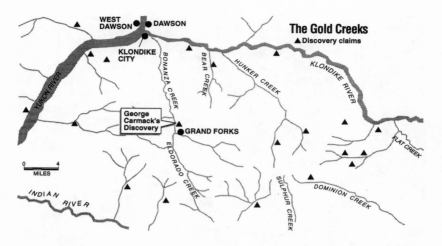

information center on Front Street across from the *Keno* is the most important place in town for visitors. Here you will find brochures, information on the surrounding area, a bulletin board for messages, slide shows, films and rest rooms.

Appendix

Regulations, Equipment and Good Manners

You will need the basic backpacking equipment for hiking Chilkoot Trail and some additional equipment for going down the Yukon River to Dawson City. The National Park Service recommends these basic items for the Chilkoot hike: Warm clothing (preferably wool), sturdy rain gear (not plastic), a tent with waterproof fly (again, not plastic), campstove and adequate fuel (there's no wood in the summit area and campfires are not allowed at all on the Canadian portion of the trail), good hiking boots that have been broken in, adequate food plus emergency rations and a first-aid kit.

Always have the Ten Essentials with you. This list has been drawn up by The Mountaineers and adapted for the purposes of this book:

The Ten Essentials
1. Spare clothing
2. Extra food
3. Sunglasses
4. Knife
5. Fire starter
6. First-aid kit
7. Matches
8. Flashlight
9. Map
10. Compass

1. *Spare clothing*. Take more than you'll need in good weather because rain is almost a daily occurrence on Chilkoot. Wrap the clothing in plastic so it will be dry when you put it on; the psychological effect of clean, dry clothing is amazing, even though it may be soaked three minutes later.

2. *Extra food*. Take enough so that something will be left over at the end of the trip. Keep emergency rations separate from the other food. One backpacker said he took dry dog food; it was nutritious but not the kind of food he was likely to deplete by snacking.

3. *Sunglasses*. They are necessary for most alpine travel and indispensable on snow and on the river. Be sure to use a keeper band.

4. *Knife*. It will be needed for first-aid, emergency fire building (making kindling) and dozens of other uses. The Swiss Army style is more practical and useful than the sabers some outdoorsmen wear.

5. *Fire starter*. Take a candle or a can of chemical fuel pellets for starting a fire with wet wood. Forget about the Boy Scout one-match edict; you may need a fire quickly.

6. *First-aid kit*. Here is an inventory suggested by Dr. Terry Mengert of the University of Washington School of Medicine.

> Butterfly bandages
> An assortment of Band-Aids
> Antibiotic topical ointment (such as Polysporin)
> Antiseptic gauze sponges
> Analgesic and/or anti-inflammatory pain reliever, such as Advil
> Small scissors
> Tweezers
> Assorted square gauze pads (more small than large)
> Adhesive tape
> Ace bandages in two sizes
> A triangular bandage, for use as a sling
> Topical anti-itch cream, such as calamine
> Fresh water (for cleansing injury)
> Safety pins
> Antacid

Moleskin for blisters

Special requirements, such as Benadryl for those allergic to bee stings

In spite of the number of items on this list, the kit will weigh only ounces and occupy very little space in the pack.

7. *Matches.* Be sure they're either the waterproof, strike-anywhere kind or keep them in a waterproof container with an emory or steel striker-pad on the inside of the lid.

8. *Flashlight.* Take an extra bulb and set of batteries. The spare batteries should be nonchargeable because they die much more slowly than the rechargable kind.

9. *Map.* Be sure it's the right one for the trip. It is always a good idea to encase maps in clear plastic for protection from perspiration, rain and unplanned dunkings. Although the headwater lakes are the only place you will definitely need a map on the Klondike trip, they never fail to enrich the experience of traveling in a new place. In addition to the map of the American portion of the park available from the National Park Service, Canada National Topographic maps are available from the Canada Map Office, 615 Booth Street, Ottawa, Ontario K1A 0E9, Canada, or from the Staff Geologist, Government of the Yukon, Whitehorse, Yukon Y1A 2C6, Canada.

The Kanoe People in Whitehorse publish and sell two books of Yukon River maps that also have interesting stories about settlements along the river. See the information section at the end of the book for the address.

10. *Compass.* Be sure to know the declination. It is printed on all government maps.

On the River

While traveling on the river you will need all of the above, as well as repair kits for the boats, canoes and outboard motors (if you use one). Since weight won't be such a factor, you may also want to bring a pair of rubber boots so your feet won't always be wet. A tarp to cover your canoe and gear in case of rain will be handy, and you can also use it to cover your cooking area if you get caught in a shower. Totally waterproof bags for all your gear—food, clothing, and cameras—will make the trip more pleasant.

You will always have a use for one or two extra twenty-foot lengths of nylon rope. Another necessity is a collapsible water jug and water purification tablets because you should not drink untreated river or creek water. Of course you will need a comfortable life jacket that is always worn and kept zipped while on the water.

A pair of pliers is one of the most useful tools you can carry because they can be used to loosen stubborn knots, remove hot pots and pans from the fire, repair packs, tents, boats and boots, and even to scratch your back.

Mosquitoes and Their Friends

You will need mosquito repellent. You'll probably use more than you expect because you may not always find a campsite in the open with a steady breeze blowing. Some places you stop will also have black flies and no-seeums, so be sure your tent has a fine-mesh screen.

Marathoners and Chilkoot

Hiking Chilkoot north from Dyea is recommended because it is the historic route. Traveling the trail in reverse is not recommended because descending the steep summit scree, the Golden Stairs of gold rush days, is dangerous, especially with a pack that is difficult to balance while scrambling downhill over the boulders. Still, when ascending the trail, watch out for hikers coming the opposite direction.

Hypothermia

Be alert for symptoms of hypothermia—a lowering of the body temperature that results in uncontrollable shivering, disorientation, weariness and possibly death. If you feel the symptoms yourself, or see them in a companion, stop immediately and make camp or rig a temporary shelter, change into dry clothing, get into a sleeping bag and prepare hot drinks.

Encounters with Wildlife

Bear, moose and other wild animals may be encountered along the trails and all are potentially dangerous. No matter how cute you may think they are, never, ever feed them. (This ban also applies to the ground squirrels that hang around Canyon City, Sheep Camp, Lindeman and all ghost towns along the river. The most aggressive ground squirrels I have ever encountered reside at Lower Laberge.)

Don't go quietly into this wilderness; make noise while hiking on Chilkoot while stretching your legs along the river. Many backpackers tie a small bell to their pack to be sure each step creates a sound. Safety must supersede reluctance to create noise pollution. (This is not an endorsement of loud talking in established campgrounds when other hikers have gone to bed; have a heart!) When you go ashore on the river be sure your presence is known. Animals are most dangerous when startled or cornered.

Never approach a wild animal. They may think you mean harm. Photograph them from a safe distance with a telephoto lens.

Keep your campsite and equipment clean. Food should be sealed in containers and hung from trees some distance from your tent so that animals will not be attracted by food odors. Bring rope and bags for this purpose.

Leave Pets Home

Don't mix pets, other travelers and wildlife. You are advised not to take them on the Chilkoot Trail, and it isn't a good idea to take them on the river. If you feel you simply must bring the critter, remember that by law all pets must be leashed or under physical restraint in National Parks. The Chilkoot is a difficult hike and the sharp rocks can damage your pet's feet. Worst of all, pets invariably interfere with other hikers' enjoyment, although most wilderness travelers are too polite to speak up about other people's pets.

They are a mistake on the river, too, because they must be kept on a leash, not only so they won't get lost or interfere with other travelers, but because of the danger they pose if they should encounter a bear. All wilderness residents always keep their dogs on a leash so they won't anger a bear that will chase the dog right into the living room. It has happened.

Everything Is an Artifact in the Park

All Klondike gold rush artifacts are of international historic significance and protected in both countries by federal, territorial, provincial and state laws. They cannot be removed from their present locations. Severe penalties are provided for violation of these regulations.

Common Courtesies

Common courtesy demands that you protect the park by respecting it and others using it. Do not deface, destroy or remove artifacts, plants, flowers, rocks, interpretative signs or trail markers. Observe the pack-it-in, pack-it-out regulations. Do not throw your garbage away or bury it. Keep each area clean so others may enjoy their visits also.

Hunting, Firearms and Customs

Hunting is not permitted in the park.

Hand guns are prohibited by law in Canada and must be left with the Skagway Police Department or Royal Canadian Mounted Police at Carcross or Whitehorse. In the United States, firearms must be broken down and encased while traveling inside national parks.

Customs and immigration laws in both Canada and the United States require hikers to report to the customs offices. Those going into Canada must report in at Whitehorse. If they take the Casey car back to the Skagway–Carcross Highway, they can clear Canadian customs at Fraser, where the railroad and highway meet near the summit of White Pass. Those entering the United States must clear customs at Skagway.

Sources of Information

For Klondike Gold Rush International Park information

In the United States

Superintendent, Klondike Gold Rush National Historical Park, P.O. Box 517, Skagway, Alaska 99840; (907) 983-2921.

Klondike Gold Rush National Historic Park, Seattle Unit, 117 South Main Street, Seattle, Washington 98104; (206) 553-7220.

Skagway Convention and Visitors Bureau, P.O. Box 415-5A, Skagway, Alaska 99840; (907) 983-2854.

White Pass and Yukon Route, P.O. Box 435, Skagway, Alaska 99840; (907) 983-2214 or (800) 983-2214.

In Canada

Superintendent, National Historic Sites, Canadian Parks Service, 256-200 Range Road, Whitehorse, Yukon Y1A 3V1, Canada; (403) 668-2116.

Yukon Tourism, Box 2703, Whitehorse, Yukon Y1A 2C6, Canada; (403) 667-5340.

Whitehorse Chamber of Commerce, 302 Steele Street, Whitehorse, Yukon Y1A 2C5, Canada; (403) 667-7545.

Klondike Visitors Association, Front and King Streets, Box 389, Dawson City, Yukon Y0B 1G0, Canada; Phone (403) 993-5575.

The Kanoe People, P.O. Box 5152, Whitehorse, Yukon, Y1A 4S3, Canada; (403) 668-4899.

Bibliography

Books

Alaska Geographic. "Dawson City." Edited by Penny Rennick. Anchorage: Alaska Geographic Society, 1988.

Bebee, Iola. *The True Life Story of Swiftwater Bill Gates.* Seattle: The Shorey Book Store, 1967.

Berton, Pierre. *Klondike.* Toronto: McClelland and Stewart Ltd., 1958.

Chicago *Record. Klondike: The Chicago Record's Book for Gold Seekers.* Chicago, 1897.

Clifford, Howard. *The Skagway Story.* Anchorage: Alaska Northwest Publishing Co., 1975.

Green, Lewis. *The Gold Hustlers.* Anchorage: Alaska Northwest Publishing Co., 1977.

Hunt, William R. *North of 53.* New York: Macmillan, 1974.

Karpes, A.C. (Gus). *The Upper Yukon River,* nos. 1–2. Whitehorse: Pugh Enterprises, 1985, 1989.

Lesey, Michael. *Wisconsin Death Trip.* New York: Random House, 1973.

Sack, Doug. *A Brief History of Dawson City and the Klondike.* Uncopyrighted. Available only in the Yukon.

Satterfield, Archie. *Chilkoot Pass.* Anchorage: Alaska Northwest Publishing Co., 1973, 1978, 1980.

——. *After the Gold Rush.* Philadelphia: J. B. Lippincott, 1976

——. *The Yukon River Trail Guide.* Harrisburg, Pa.: Stackpole, 1975.

Schwatka, Frederick. *A Summer in Alaska.* Philadelphia: John Y. Huber Co, 1891.

Wright, Allen A. *Prelude to Bonanza.* Sidney, British Columbia: Gray's Publishing Ltd., 1976.

Magazines

Alaska Magazine
The Beaver
Northwest Living

Newspapers

Seattle *Post-Intelligencer*
Seattle *Times*
Whitehorse *Star*

Unpublished Material

Bearss, Edwin C. "Proposed Klondike Gold Rush National Historical Park: Historic Resource Study." Washington D.C.: National Park Service, 1970.

Gurcke, Karl. "Cultural Resources along the Chilkoot Trail: Trailhead to Finnegan's Point; Finnegan's Point to Canyon City" (and some work in Dyea).

Norris, Frank. "Draft of Chilkoot Trail Historical Structure Report: Knockdown Boats; Finnegan's Point; Canyon City; Pleasant Camp; Sheep Camp; Stone House; Site of the Palm Sunday Avalanche; the Scales."

Index